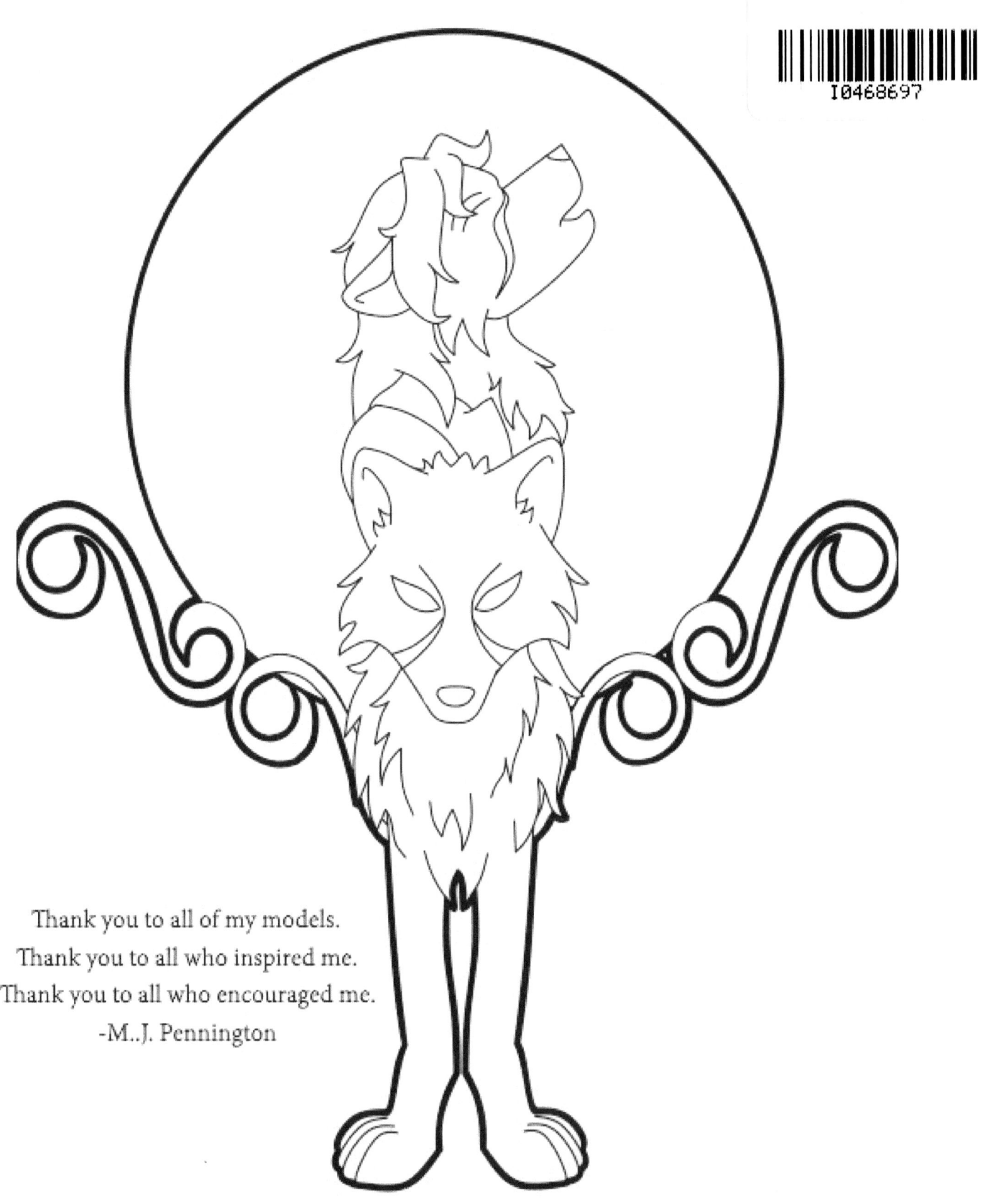

Thank you to all of my models.
Thank you to all who inspired me.
Thank you to all who encouraged me.
-M..J. Pennington

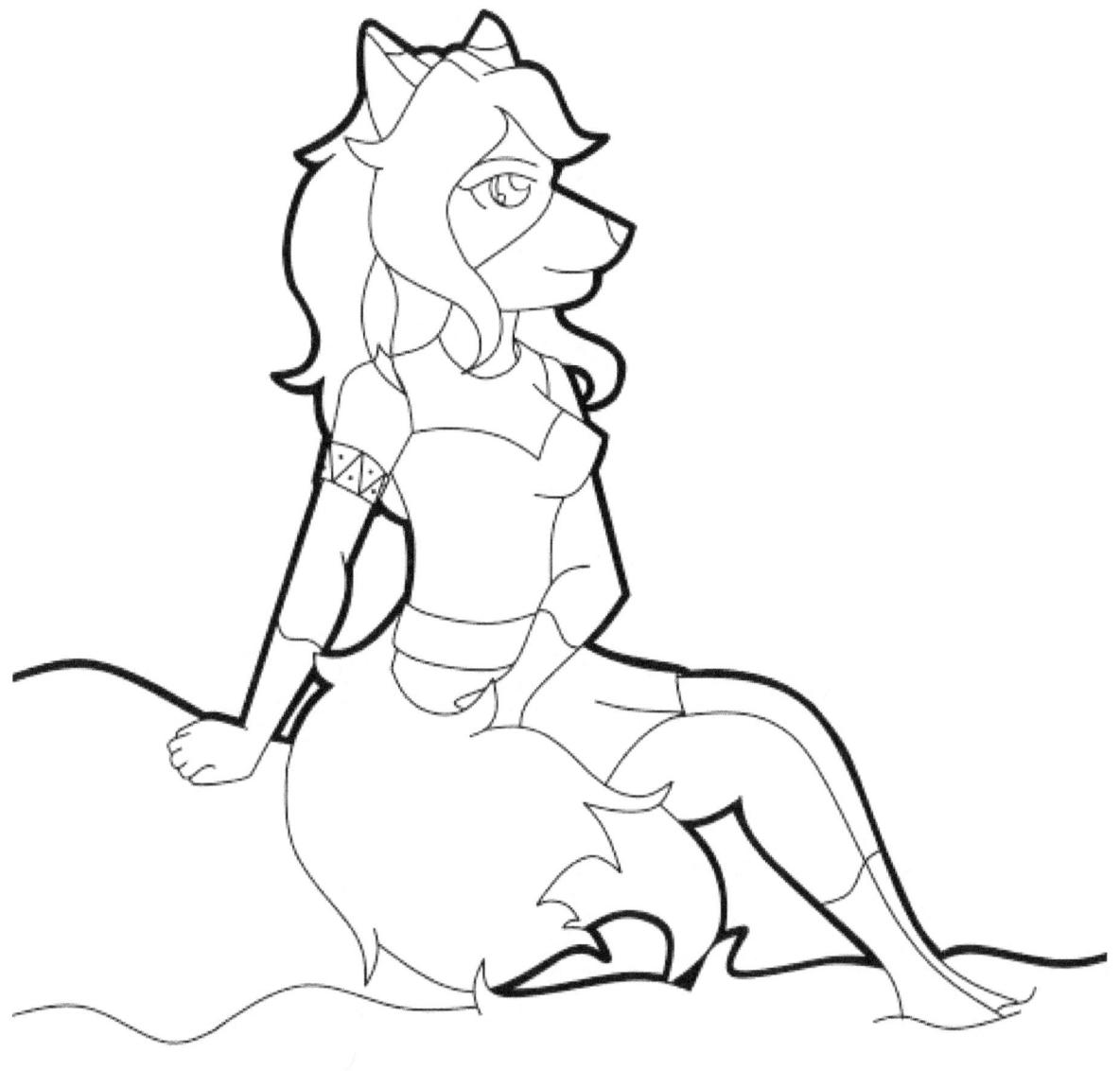

Fox by the river © 2016 M.J. Pennington/ Orange Angels Studio

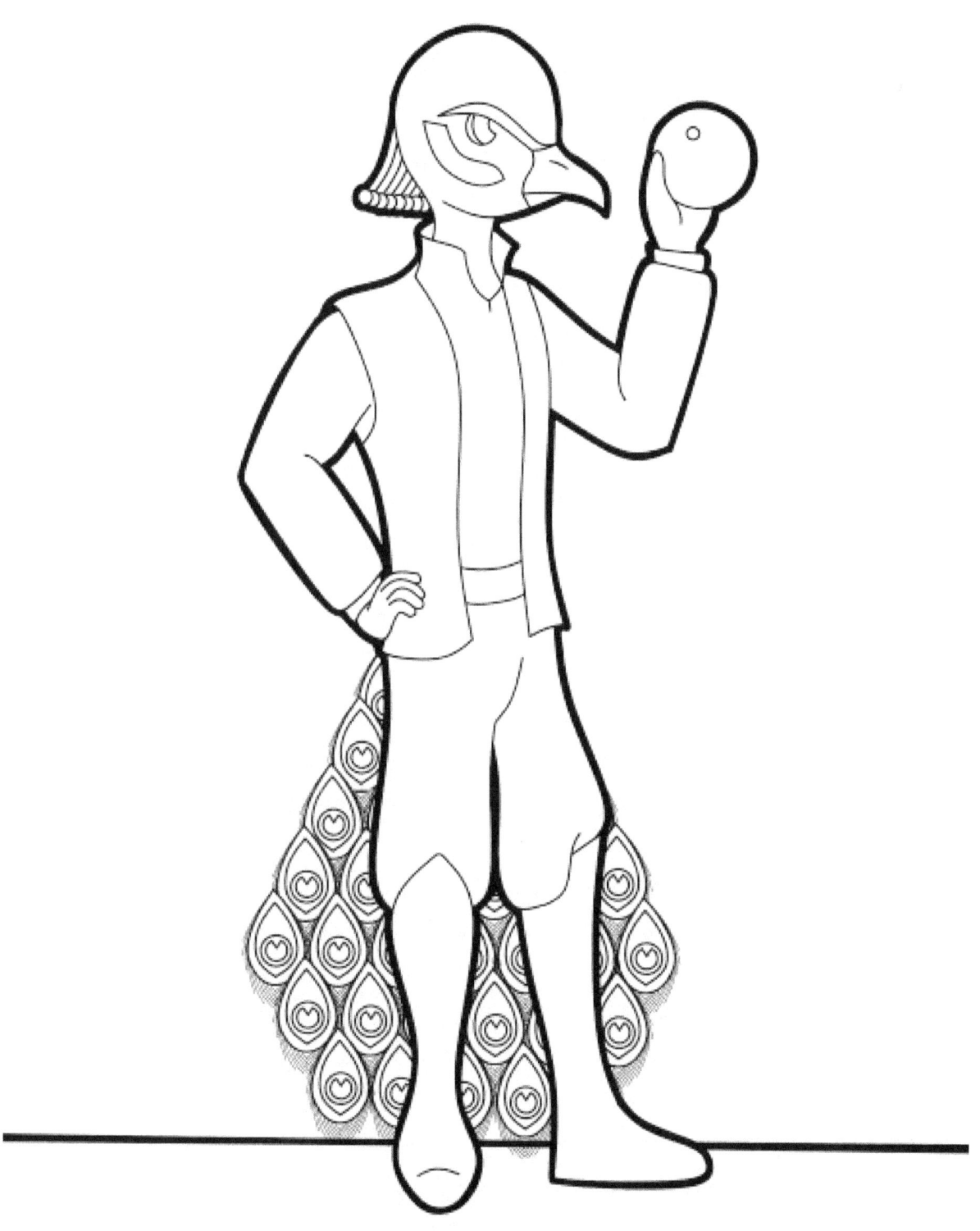

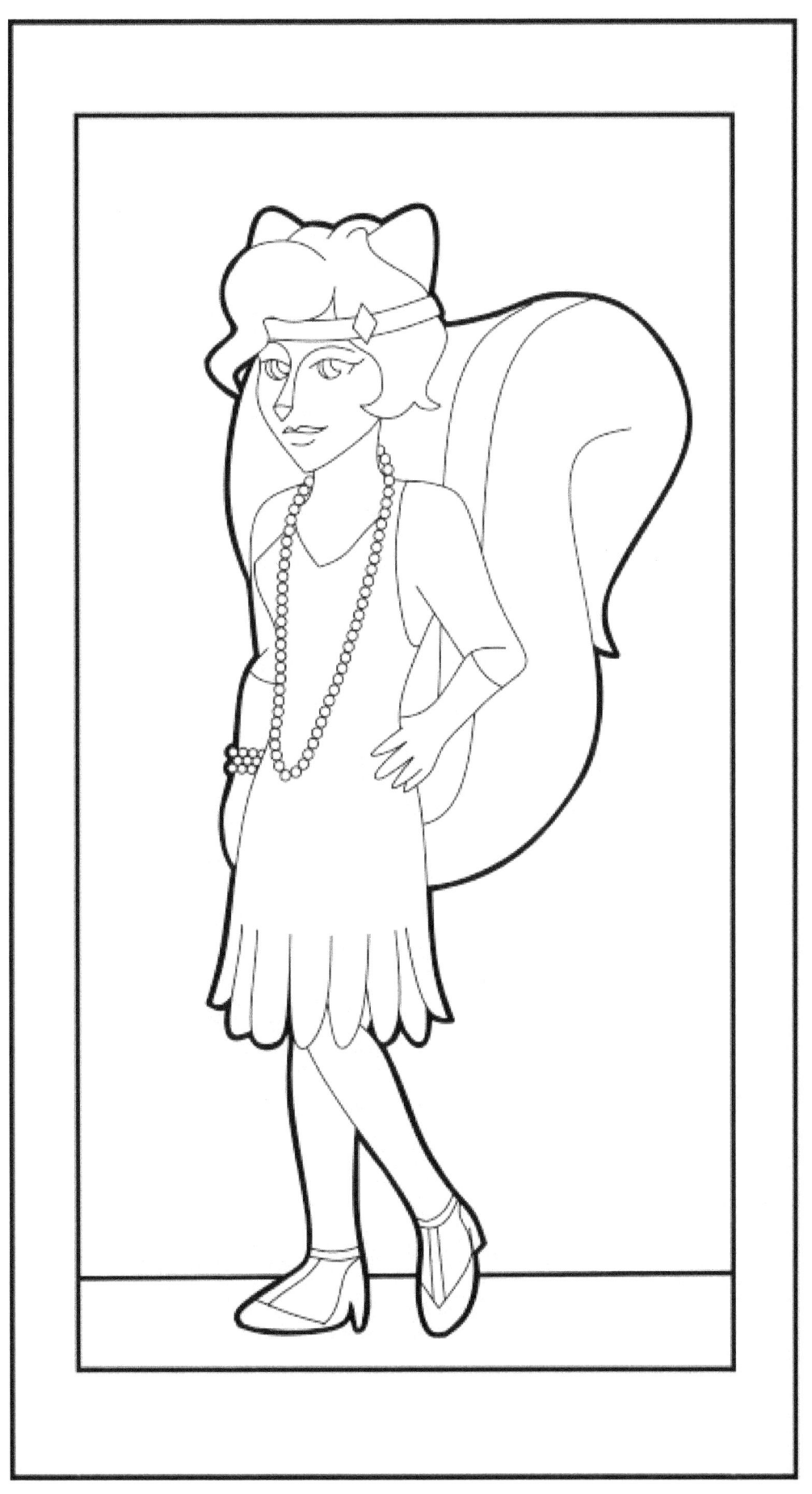

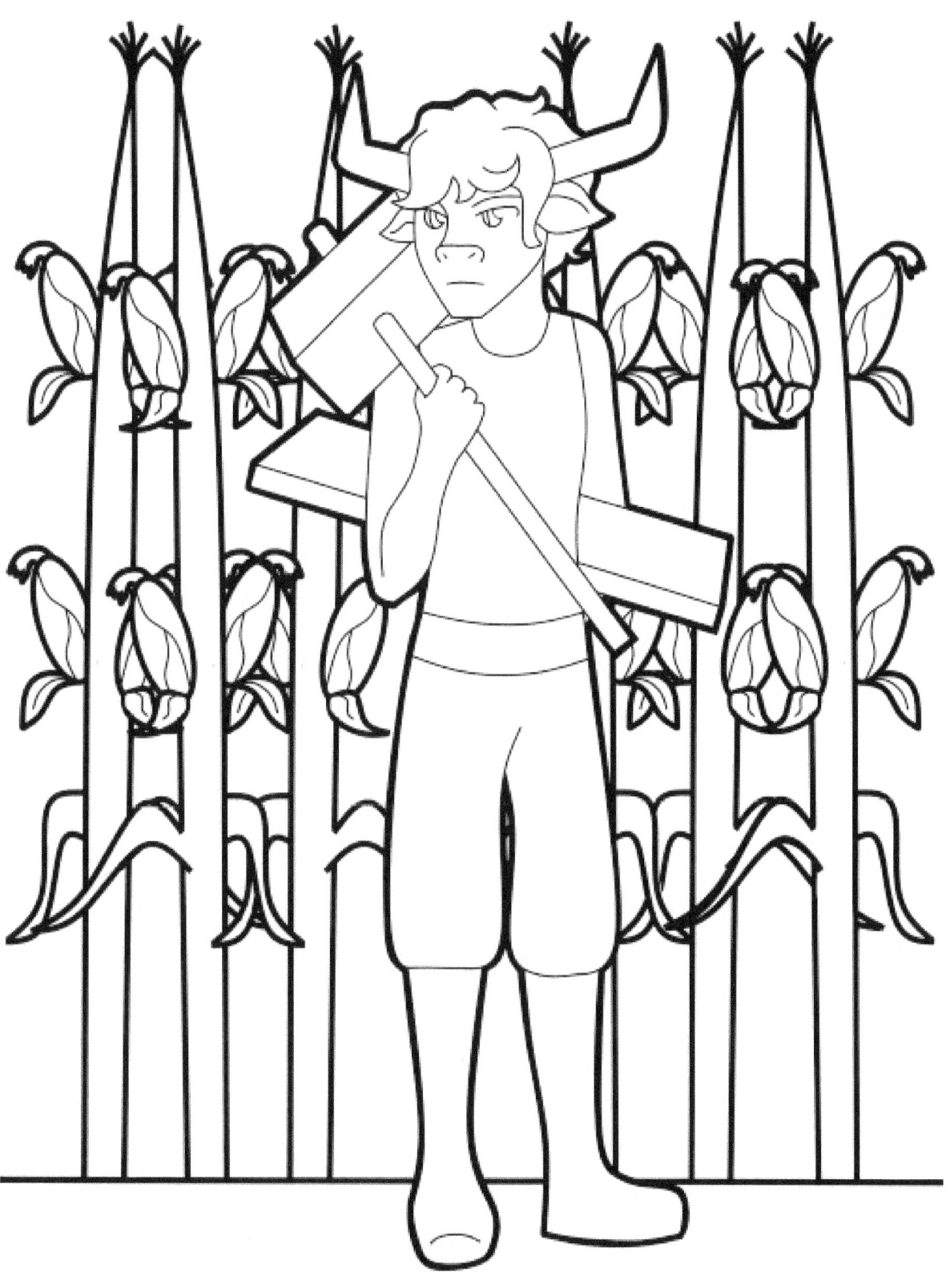

The hard worker © 2016 M.J. Pennington/ Orange Angels Studio

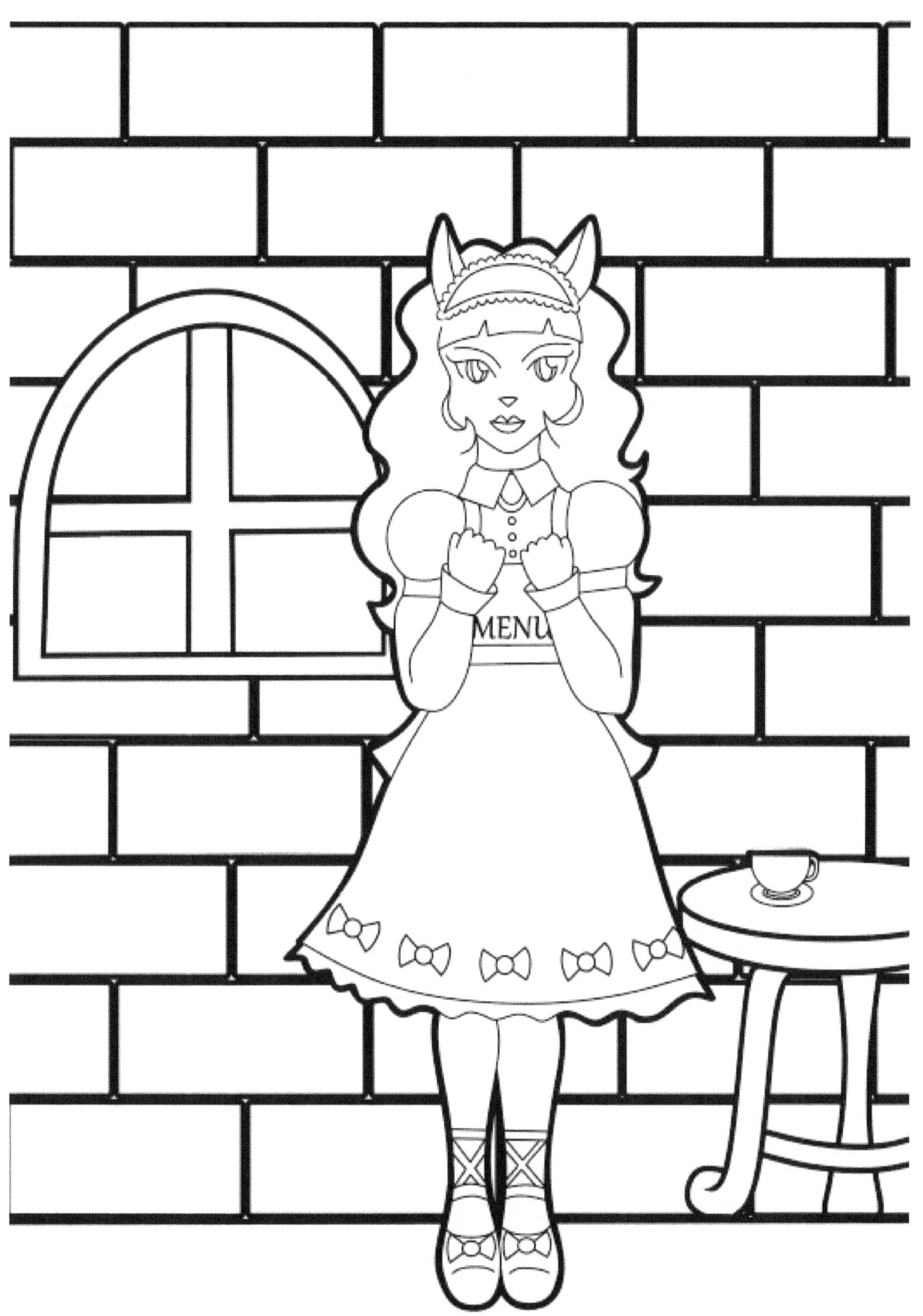

Welcome to the Llama Cafe © 2016 M.J. Pennington/ Orange Angels Studio

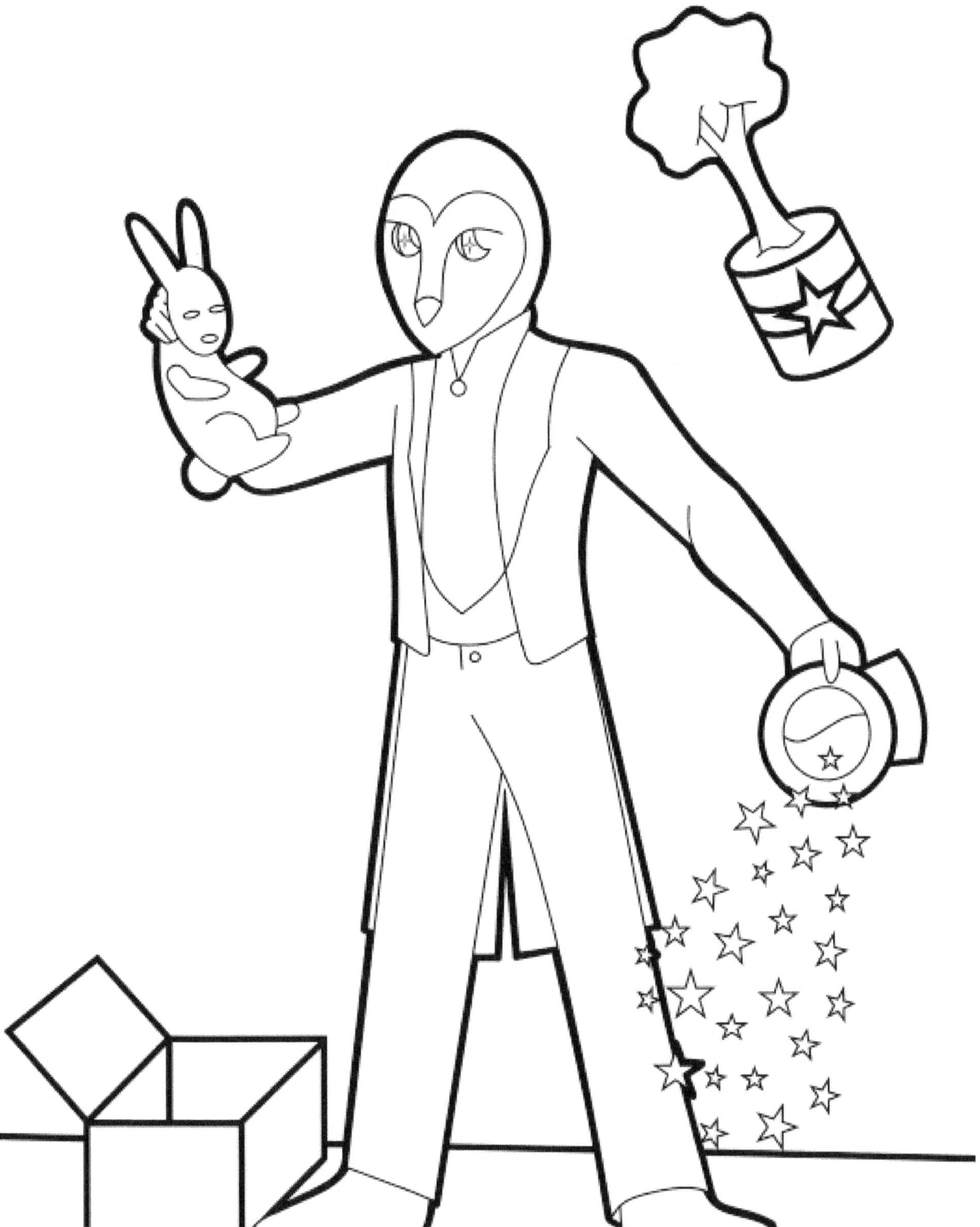

A true Magician never reveals his tricks

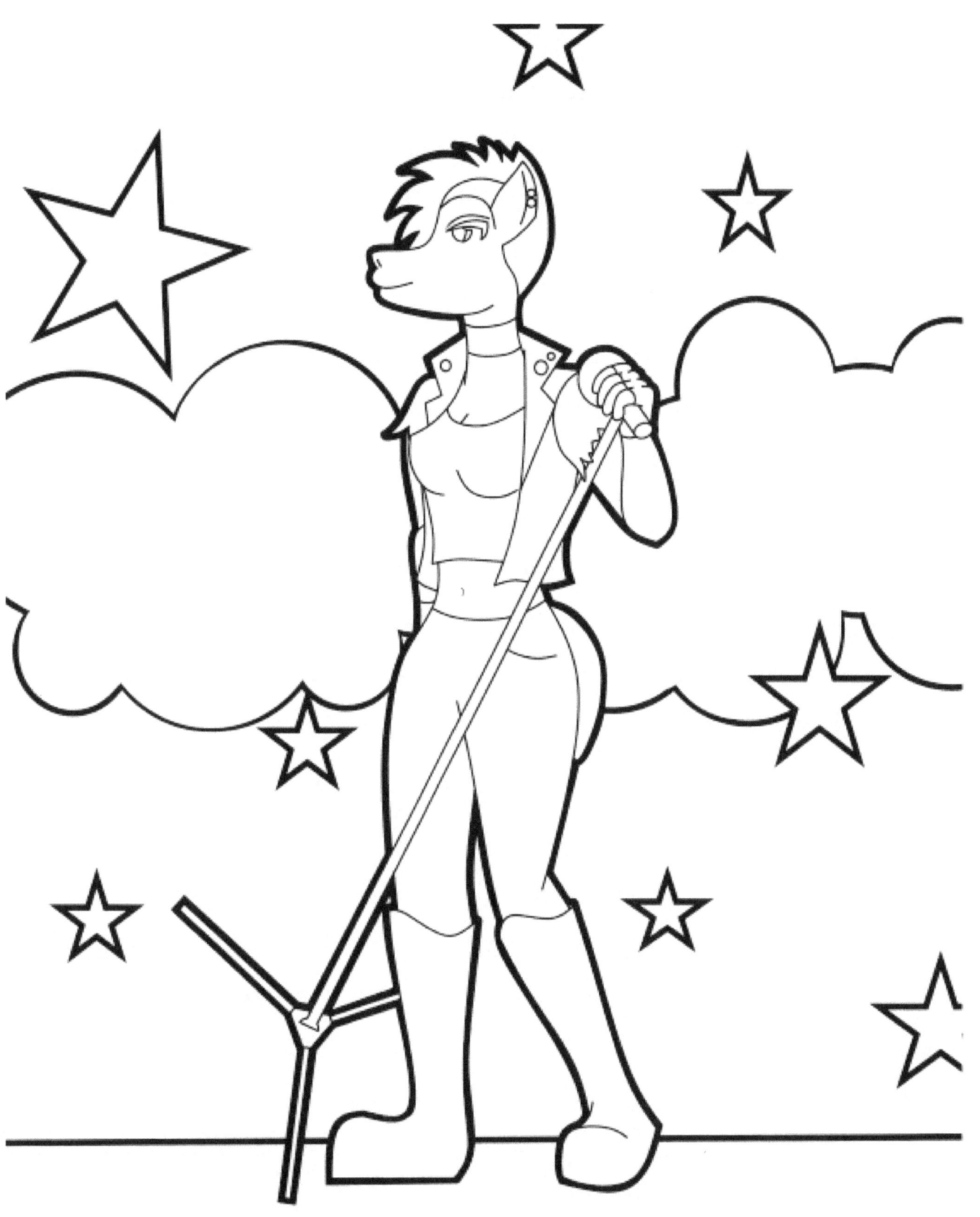

Now presenting the Shaved Alpacas © 2016 M.J. Pennington/ Orange Angels Studio

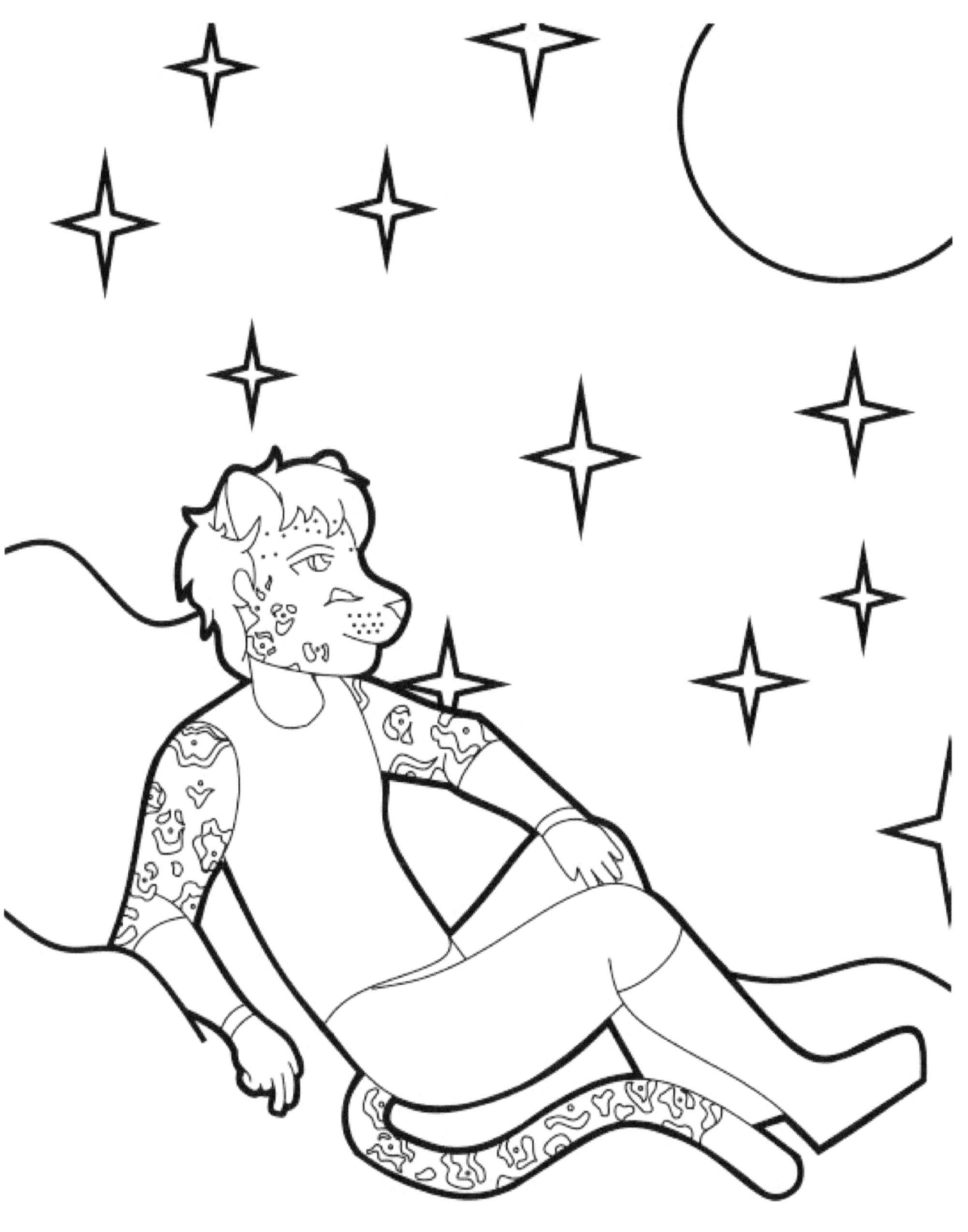

Jaque lounging under the stars © 2016 M.J. Pennington/ Orange Angels Studio

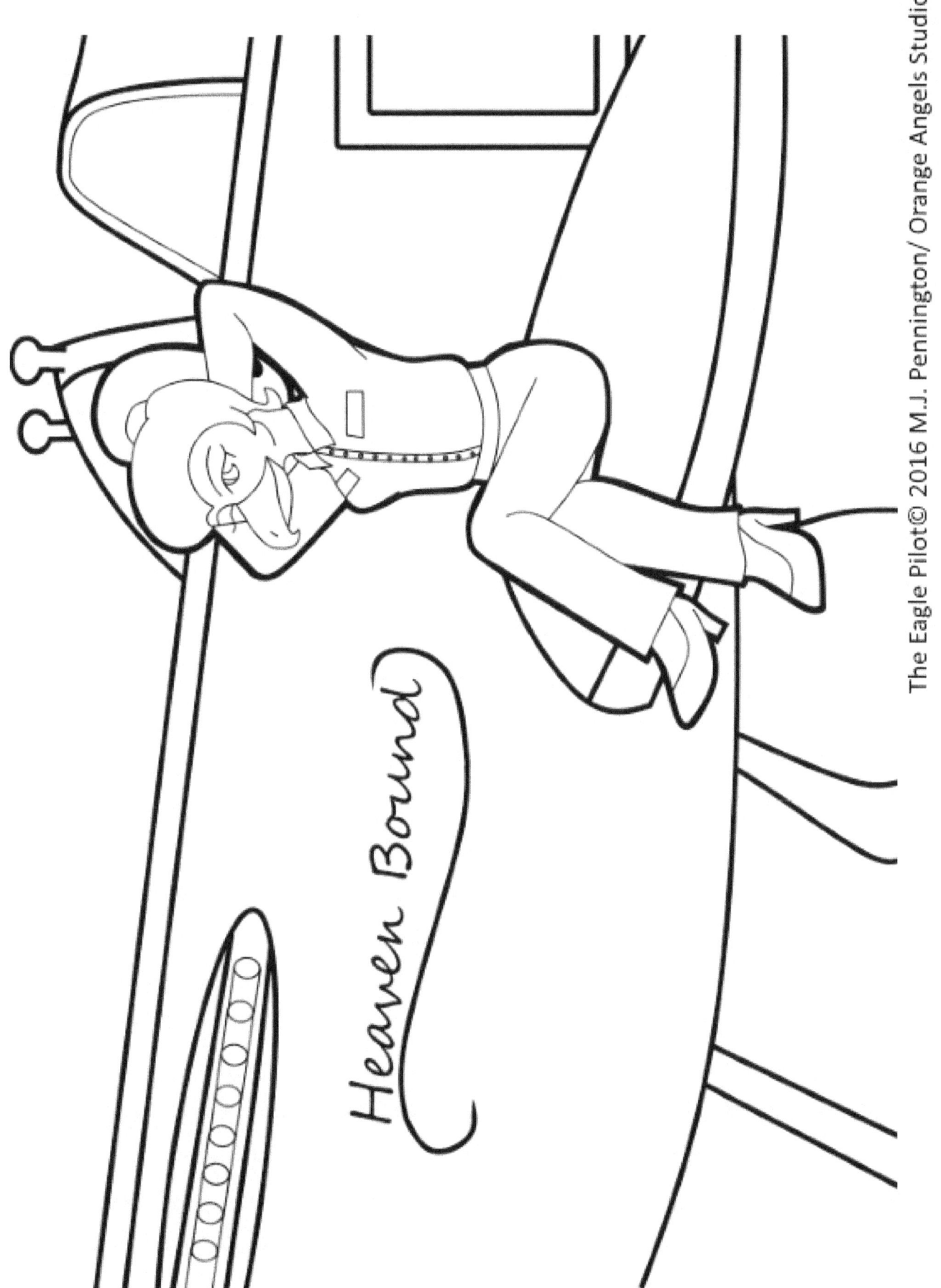

Heaven Bound

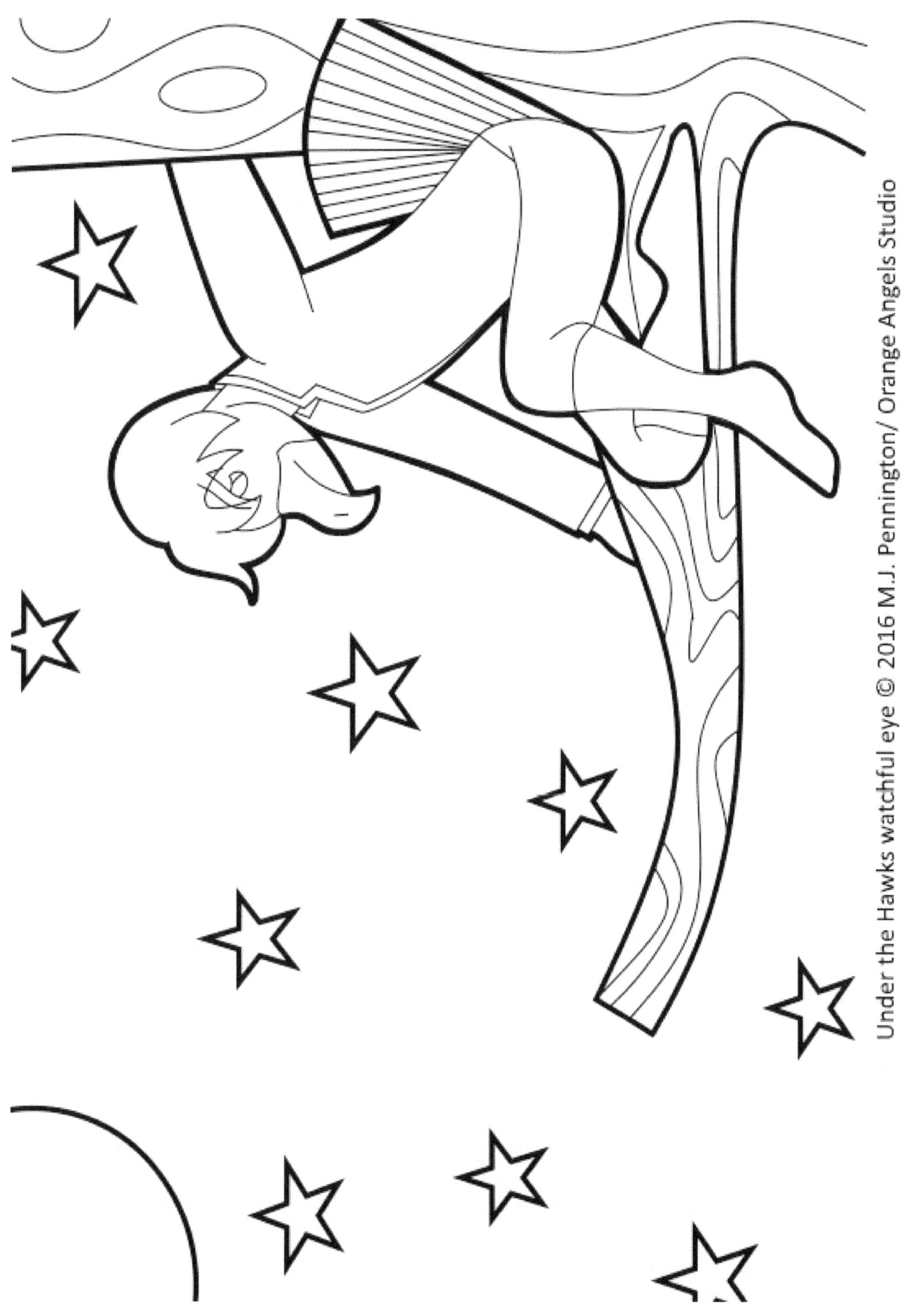

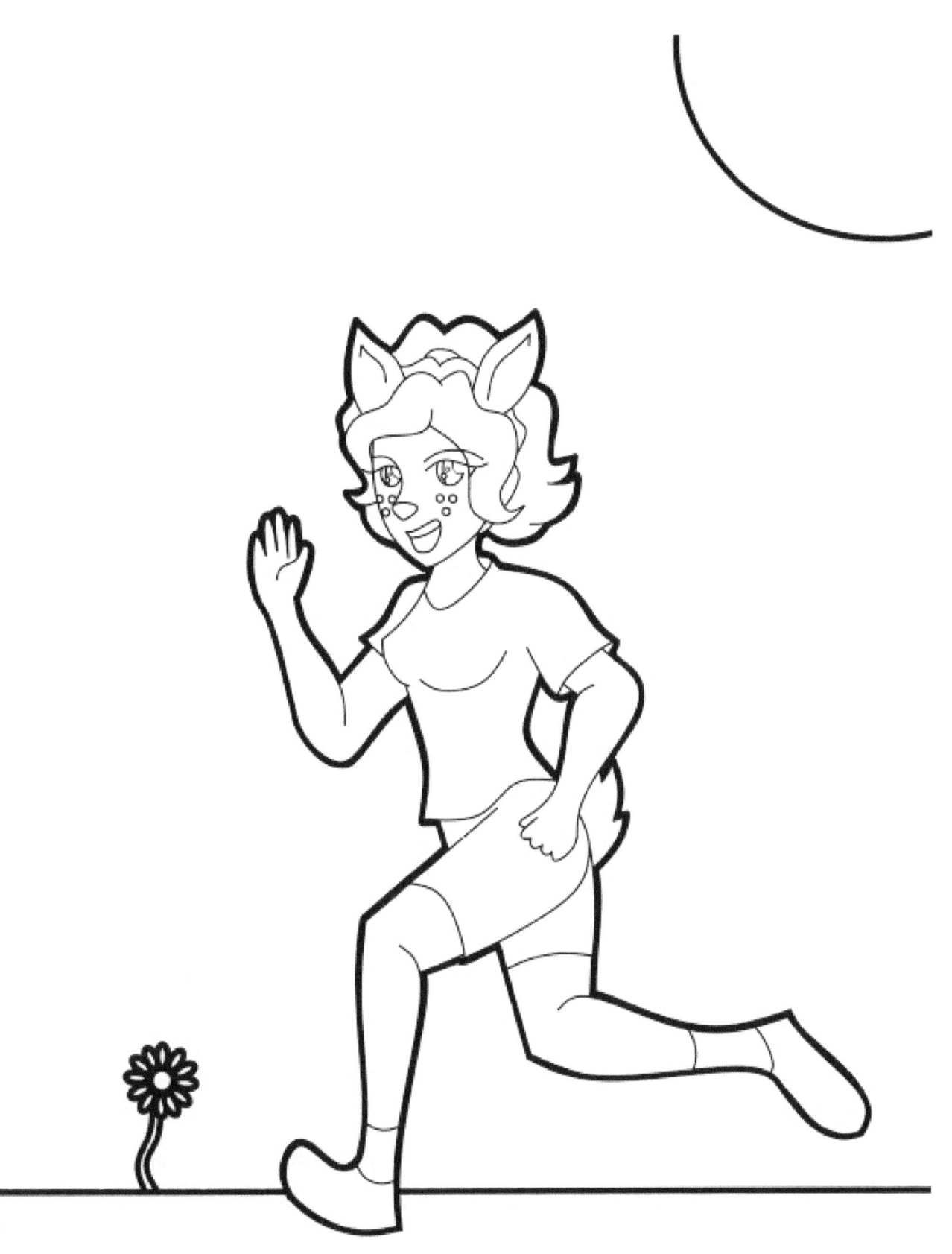

The Happy Runner © 2016 M.J. Pennington/ Orange Angels Studio

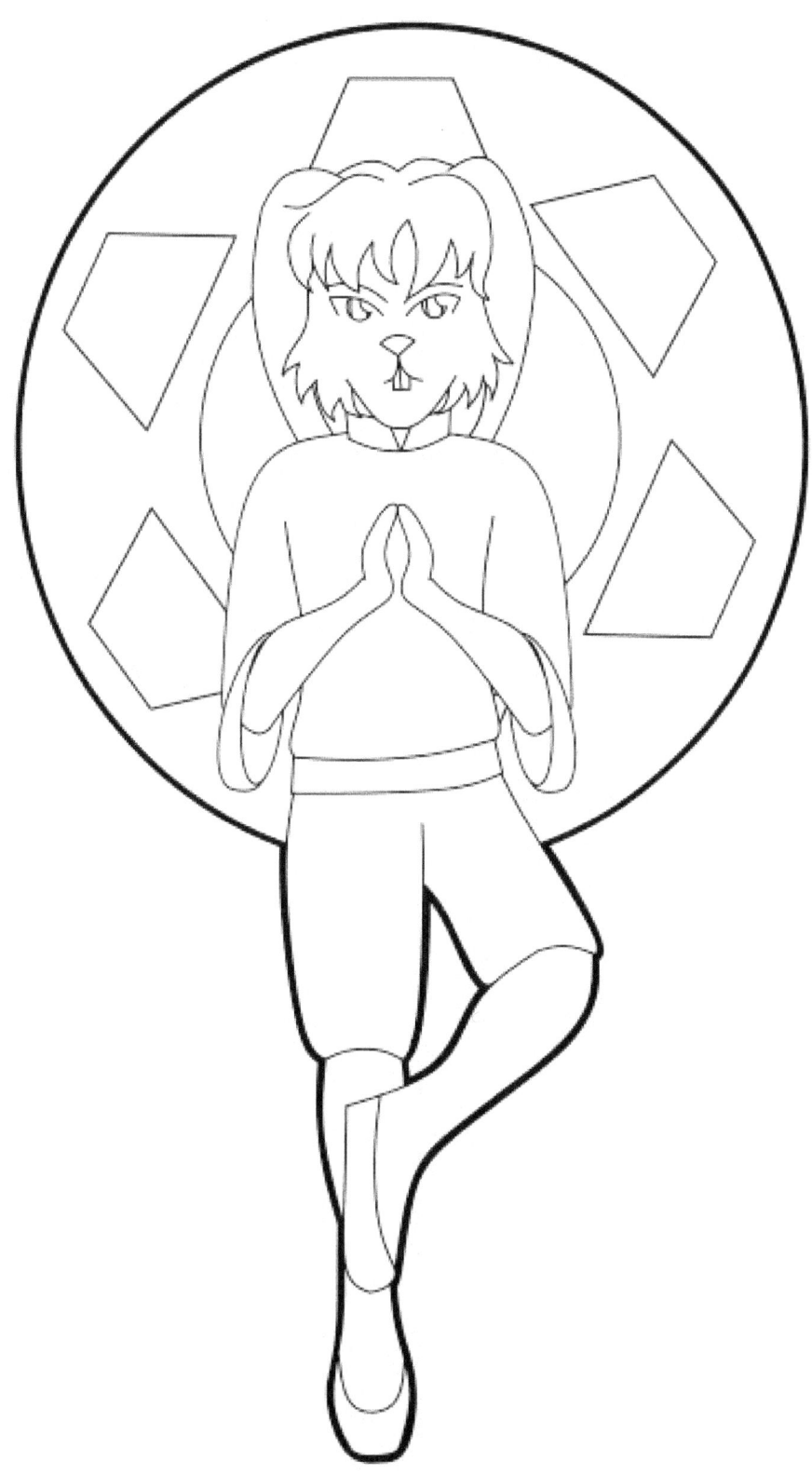

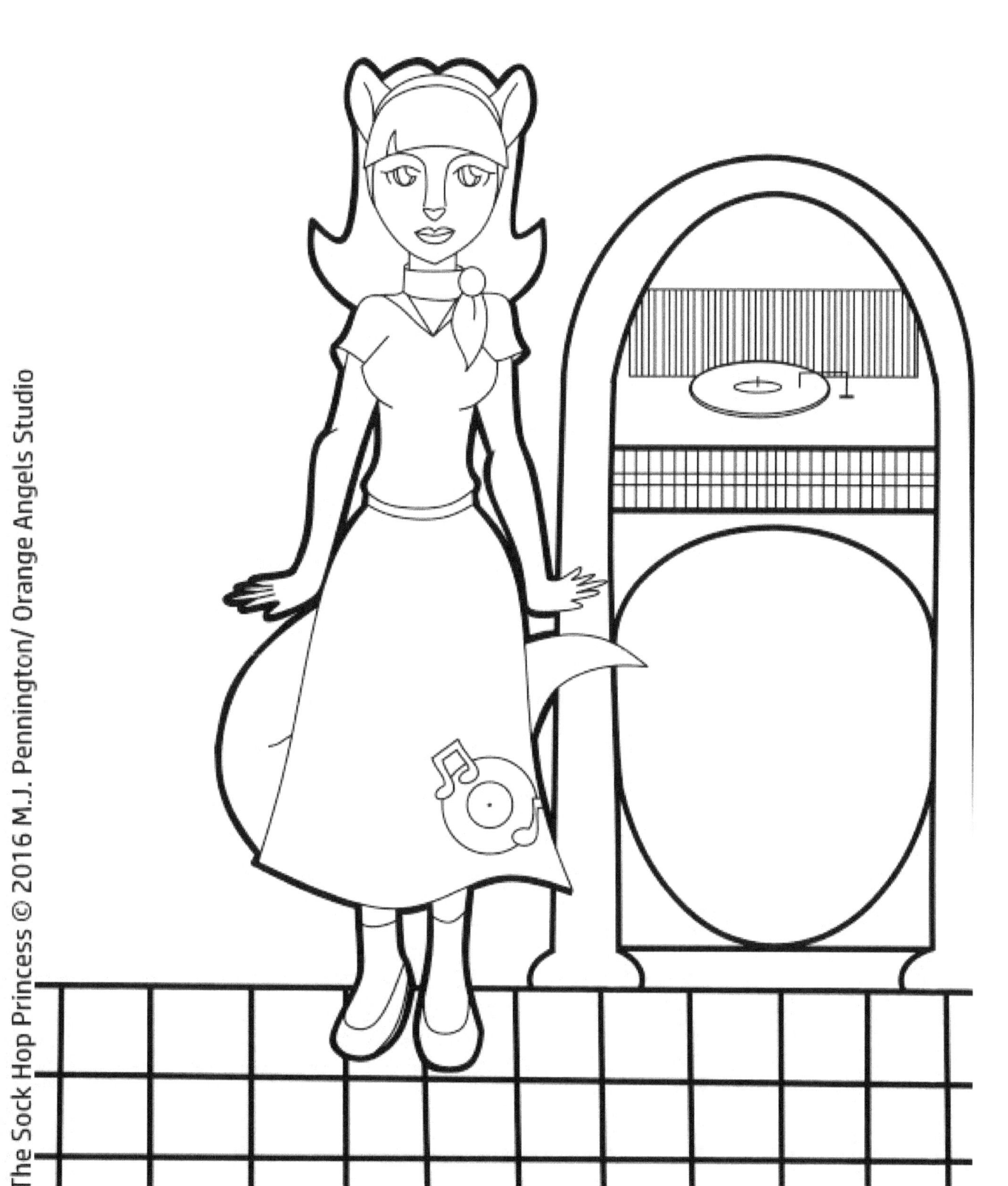

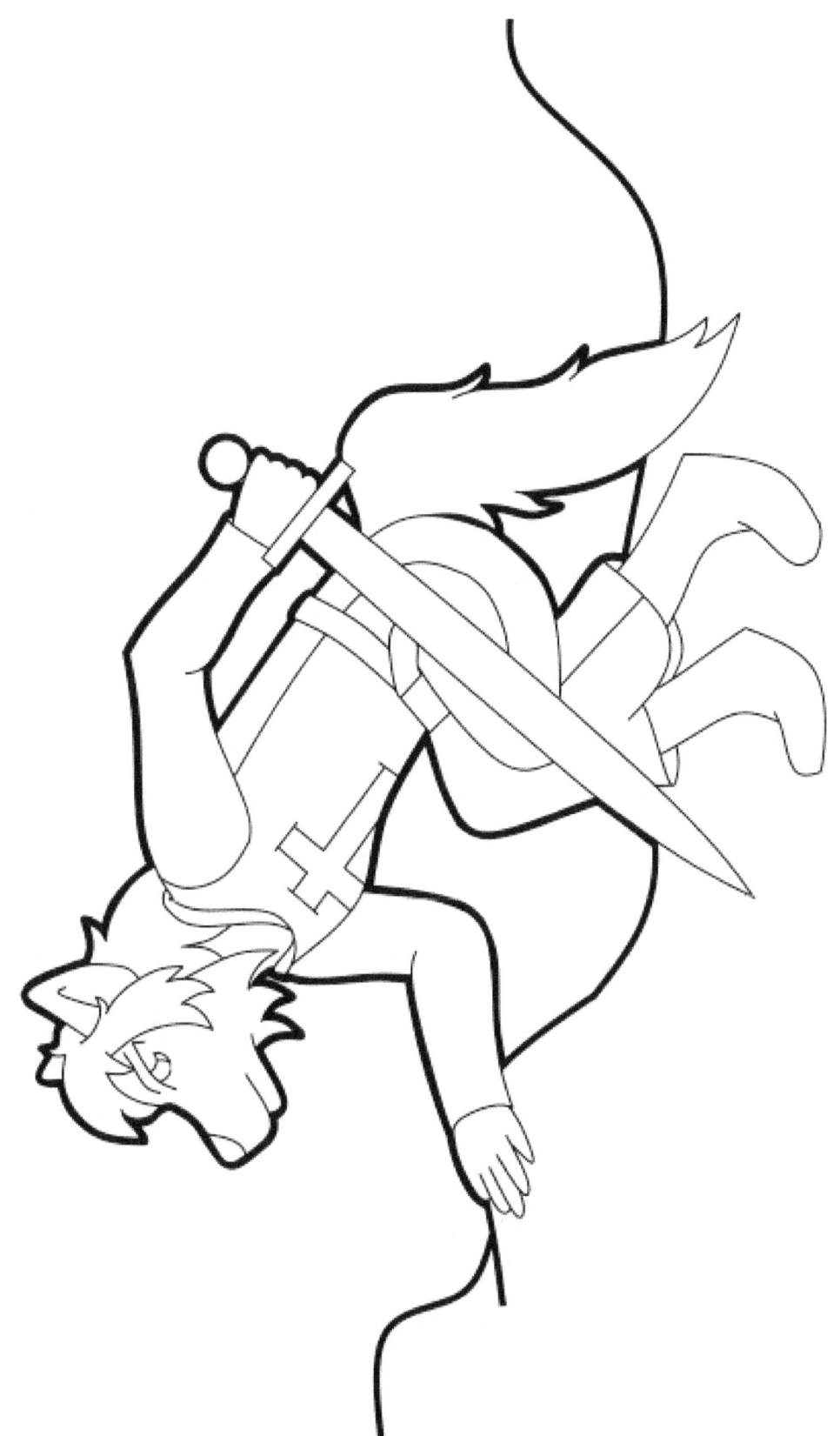

True Queen of the Nile © 2016 M.J. Pennington/ Orange Angels Studio

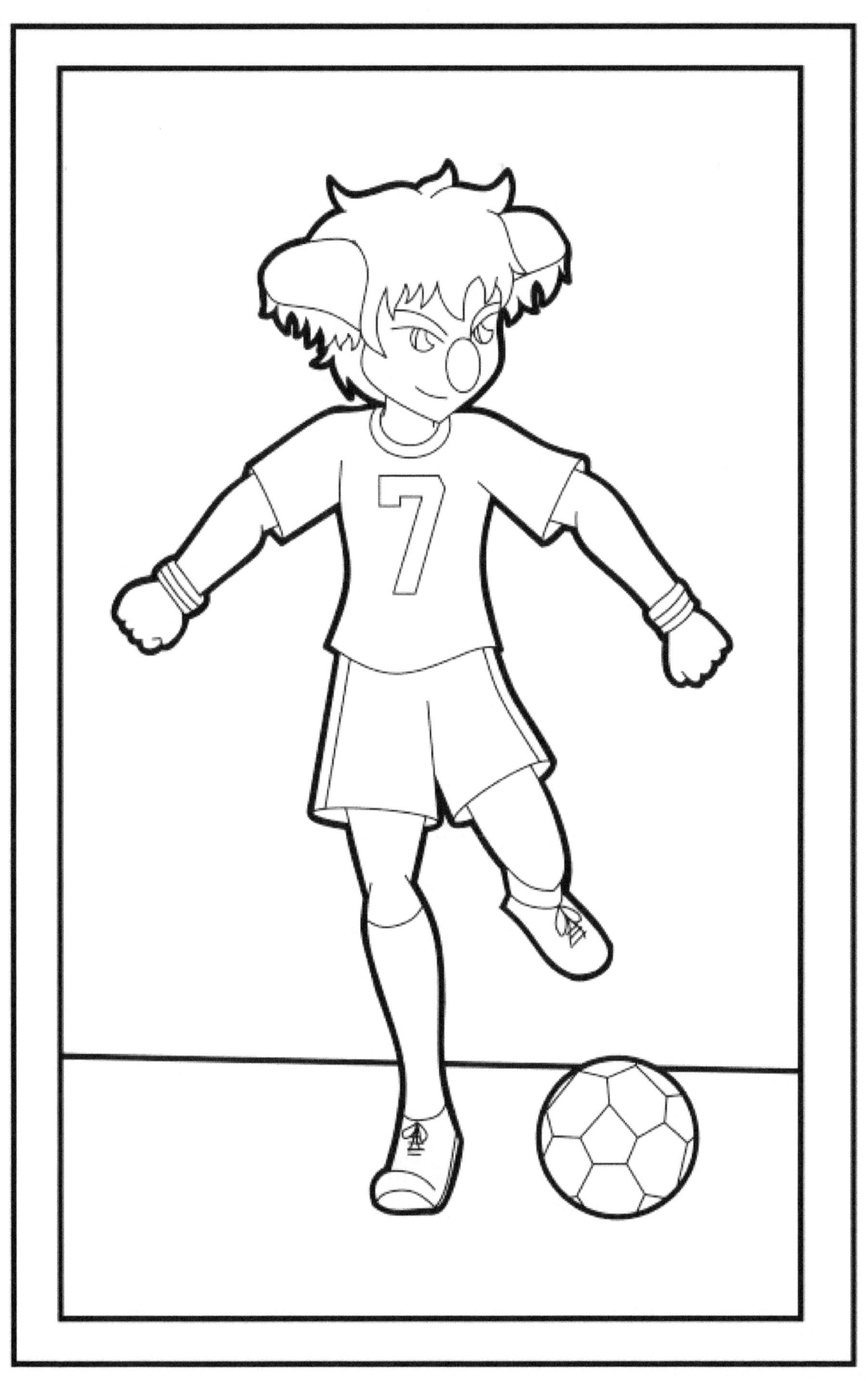

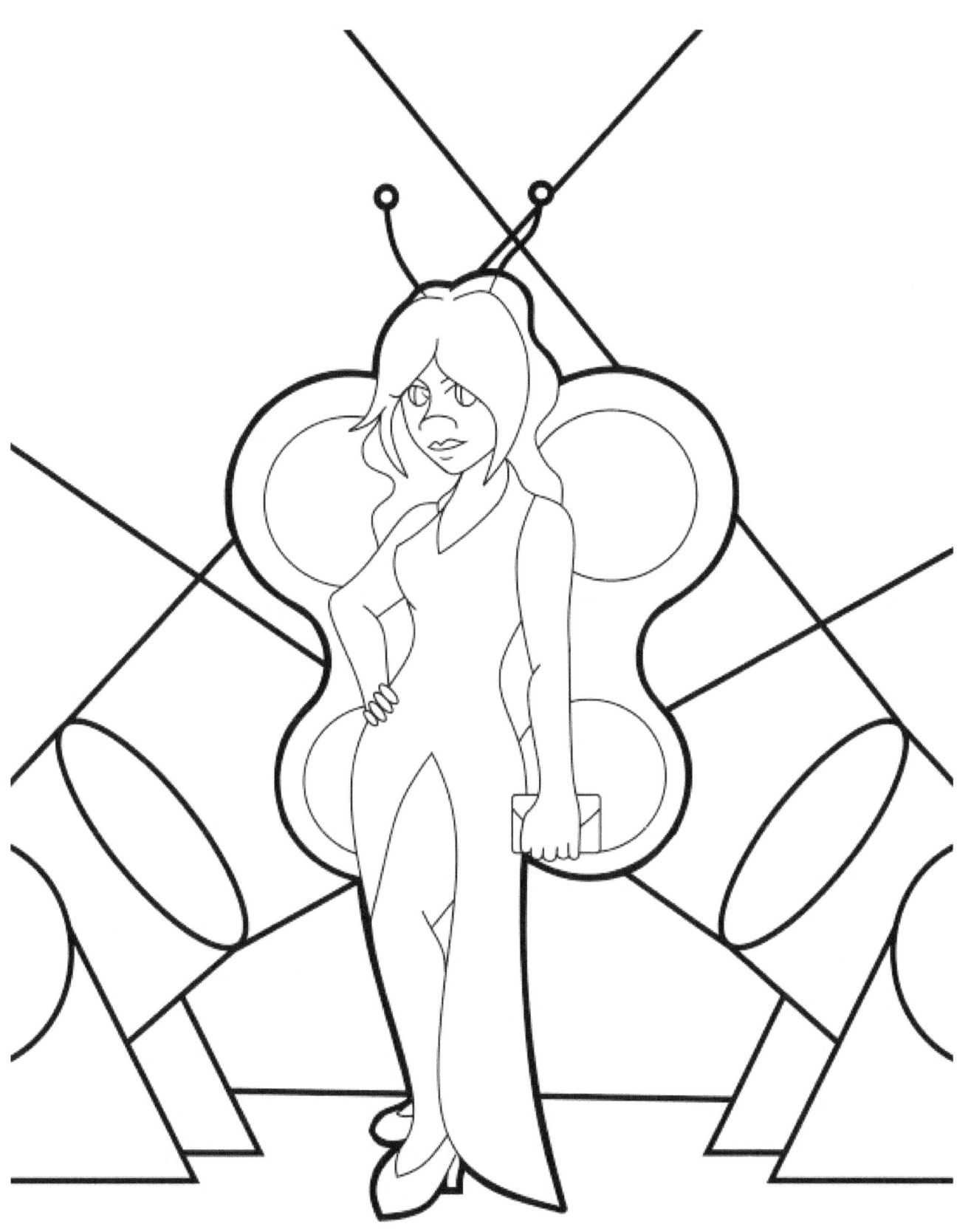

Her Time To Shine © 2016 M.J. Pennington/ Orange Angels Studio

Come see the AMAZING
•CHARLAMAGE•

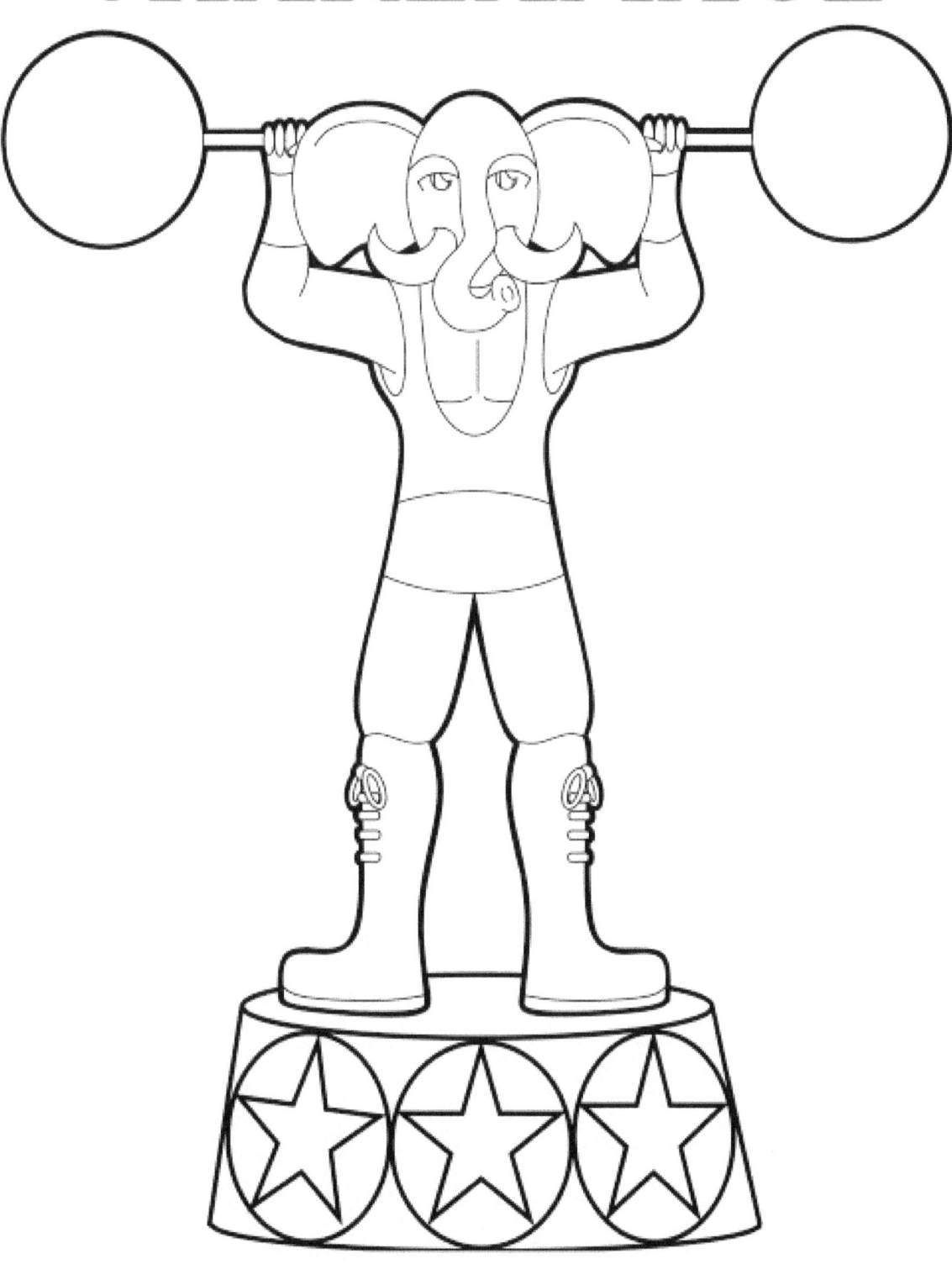

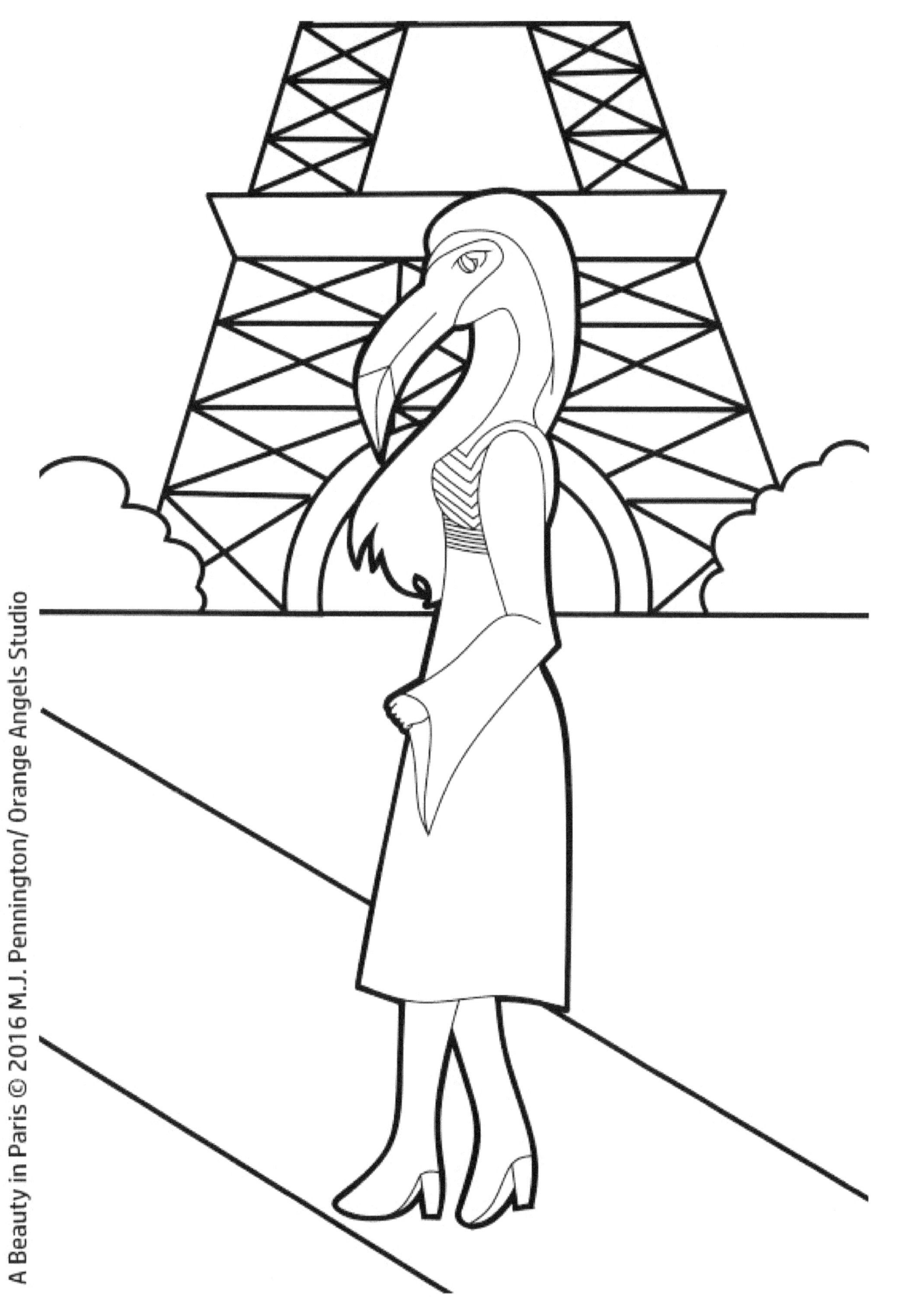

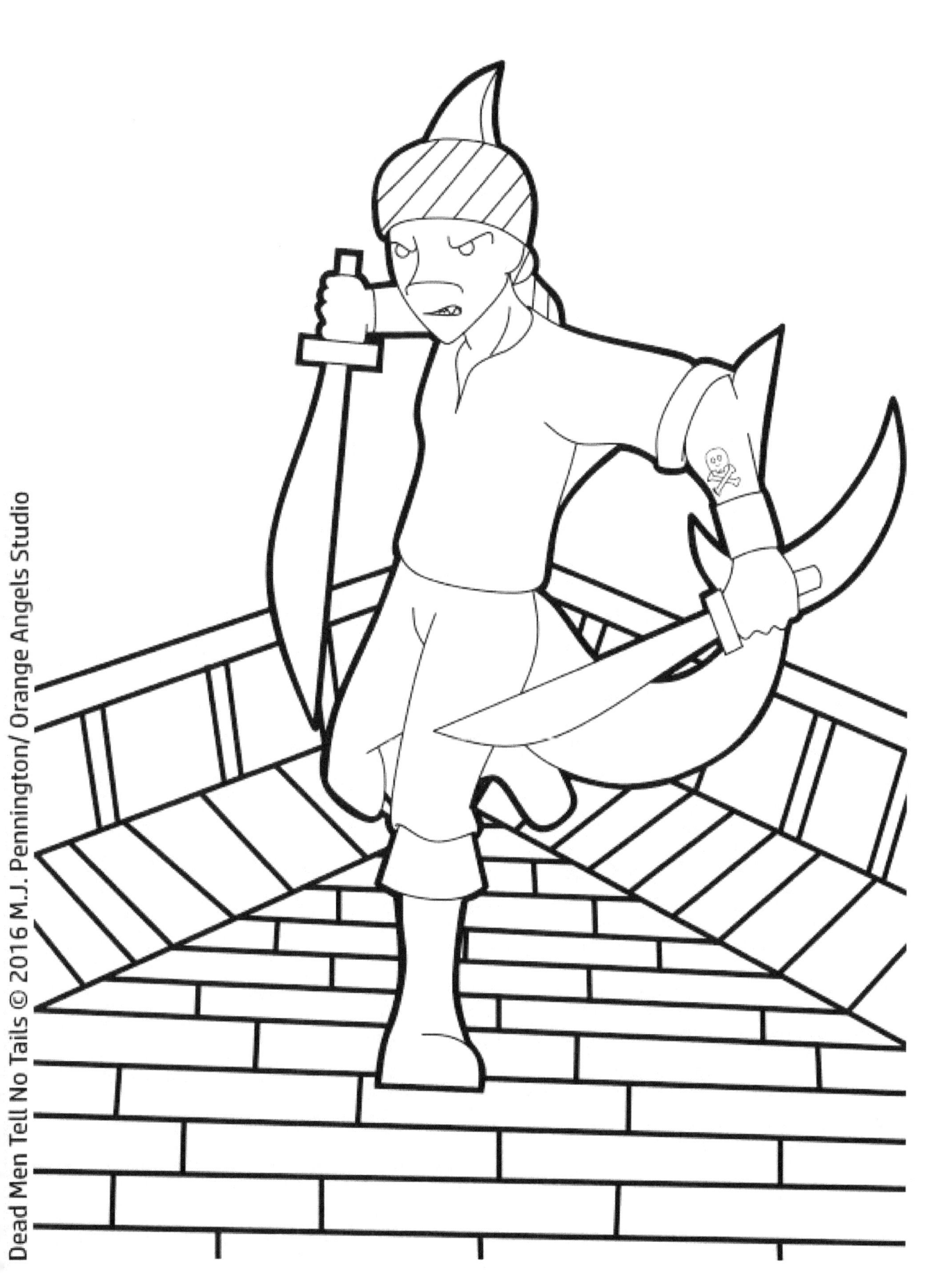

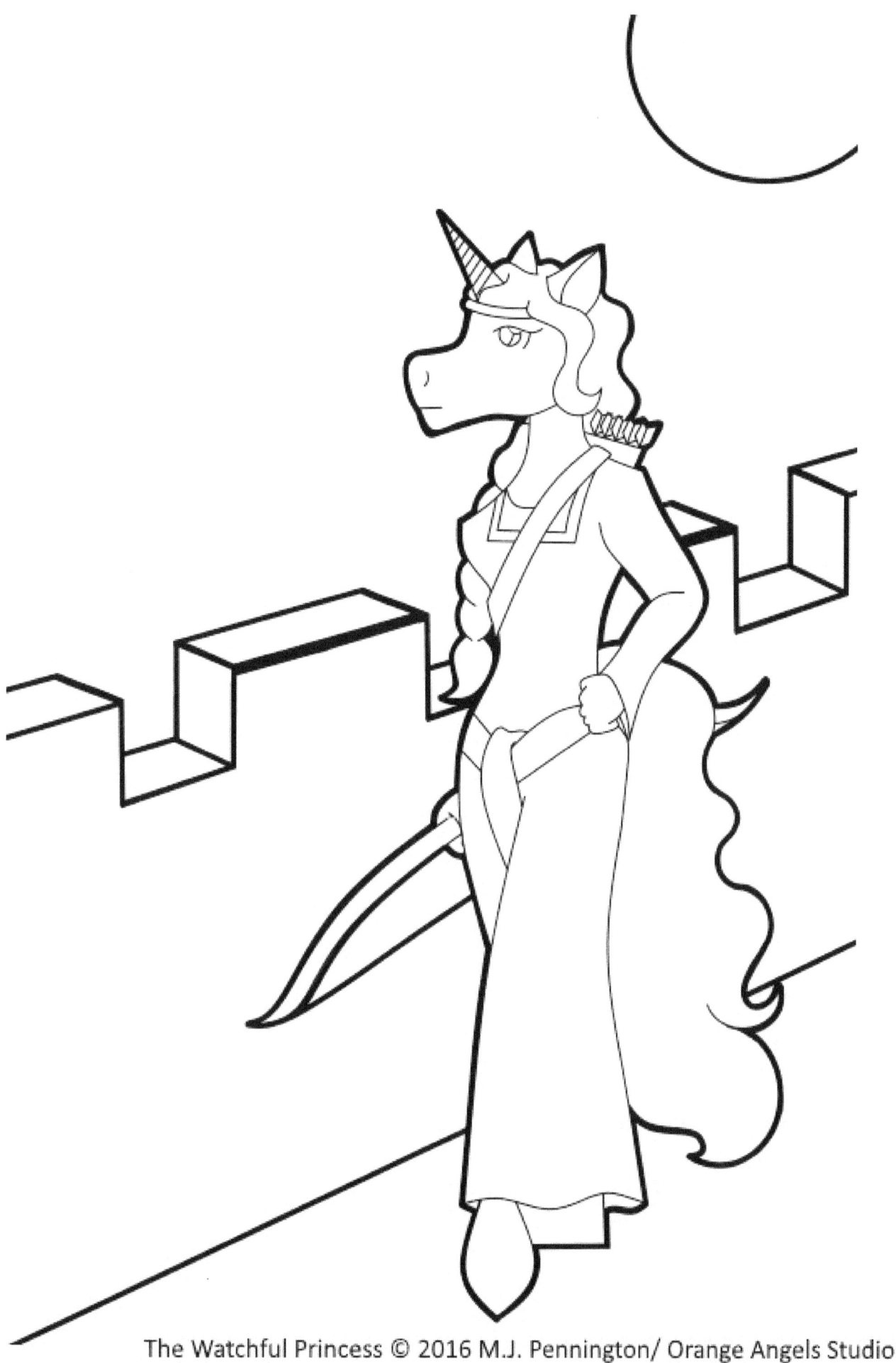

The Watchful Princess © 2016 M.J. Pennington/ Orange Angels Studio

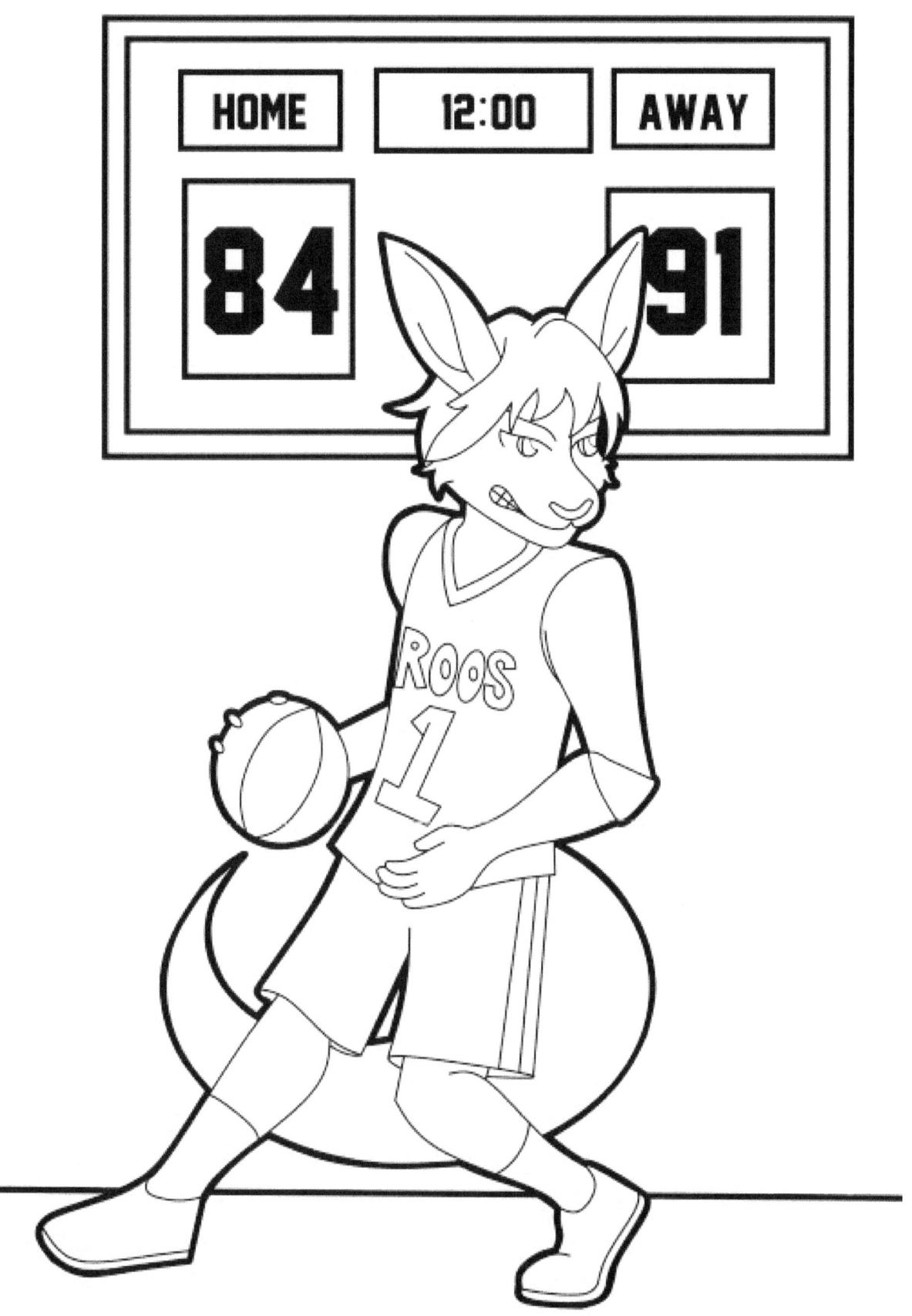

Go for the win Joey! © 2016 M.J. Pennington/ Orange Angels Studio

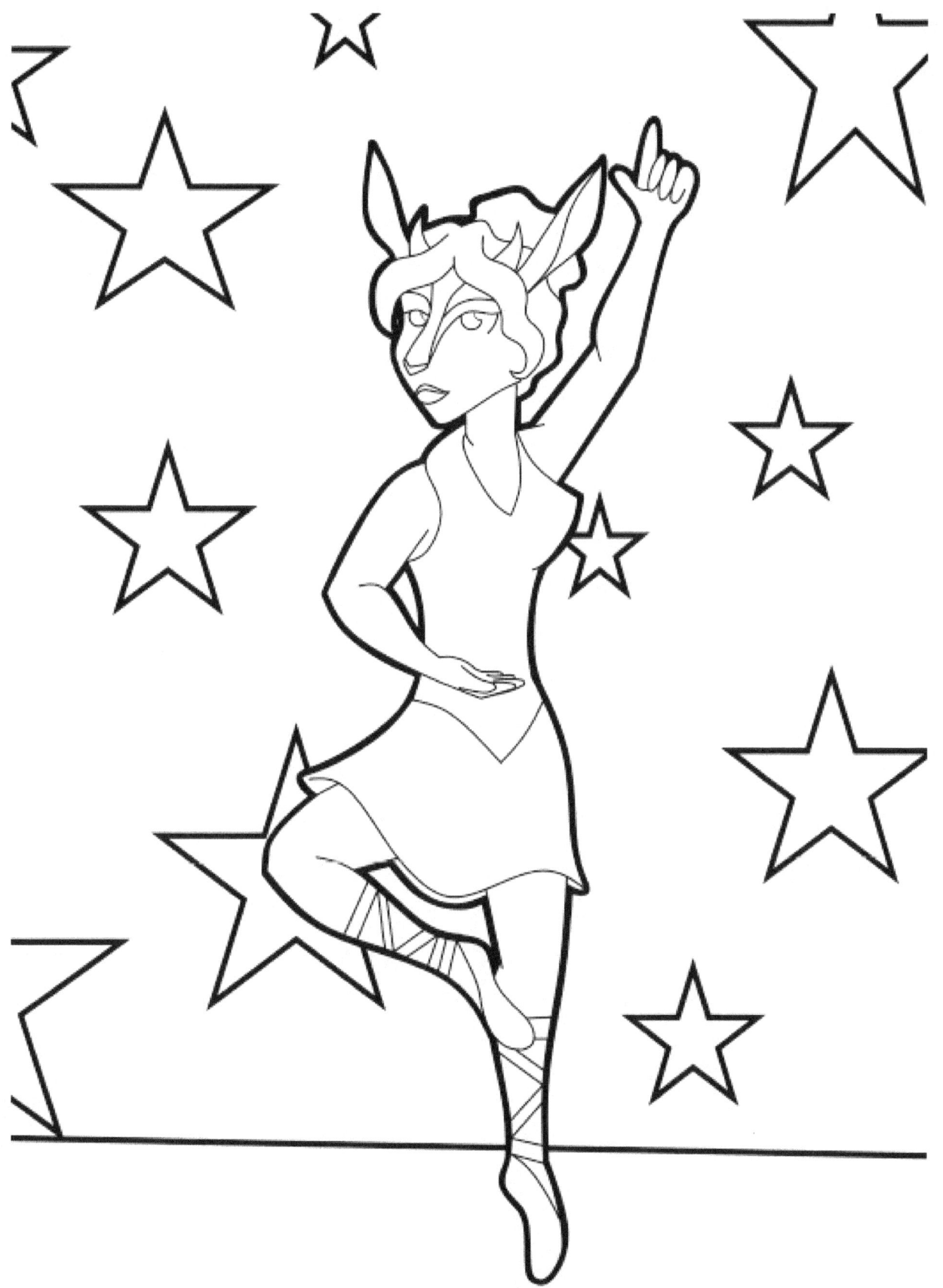

Graceful Gazelle © 2016 M.J. Pennington/ Orange Angels Studio

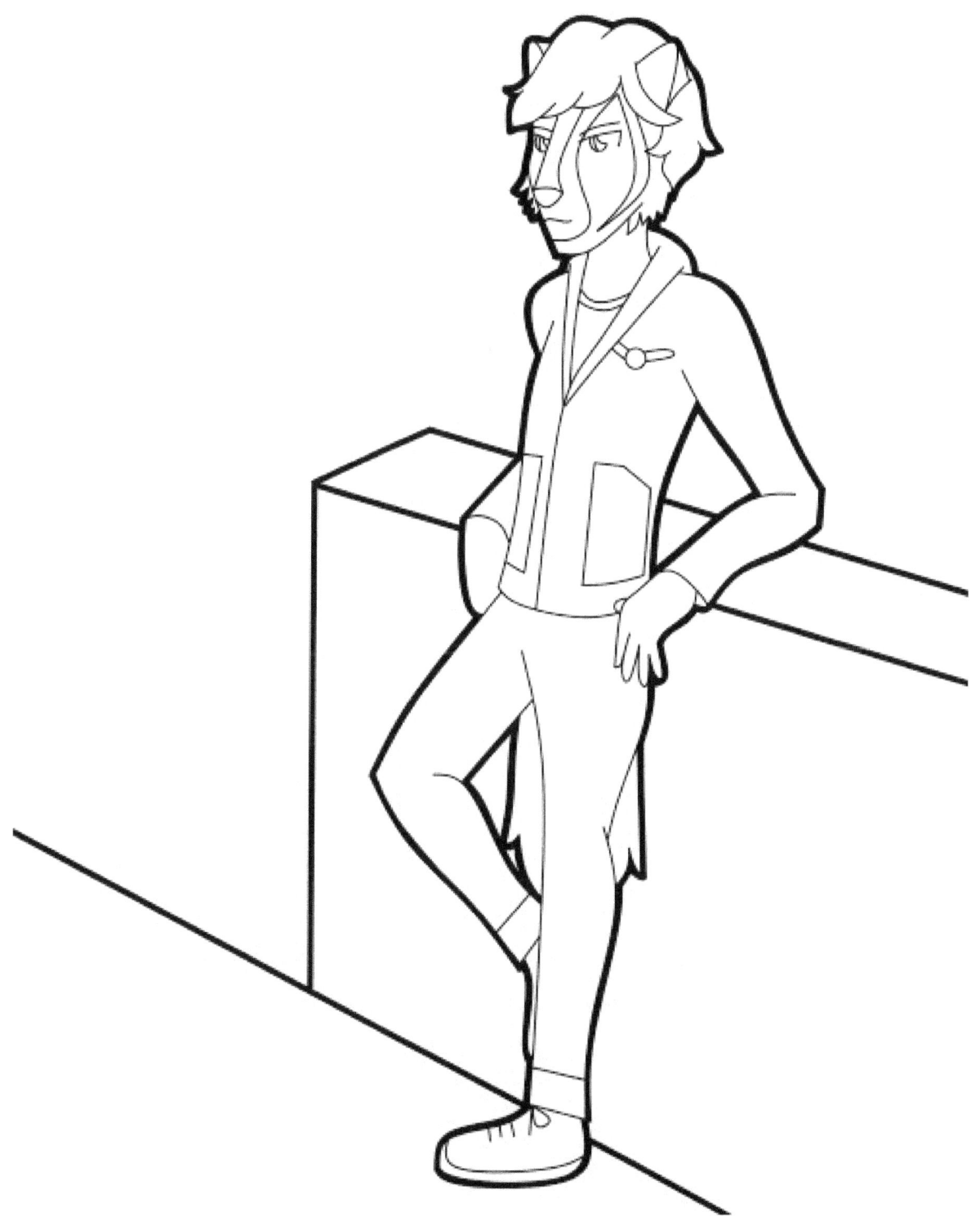

Honey Badger Don't Care © 2016 M.J. Pennington / Orange Angels Studio

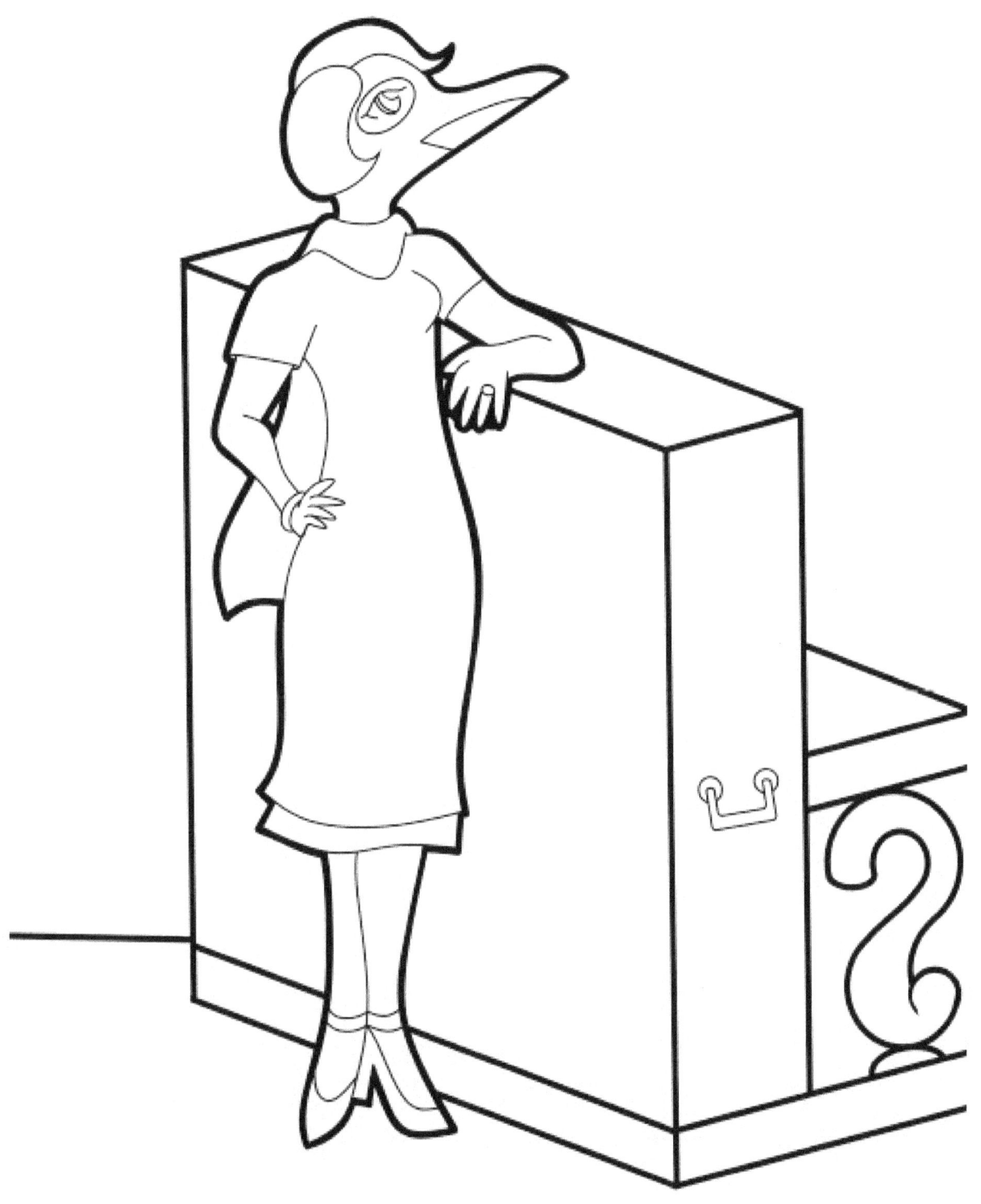

Follow your Dream Miss Penguin © 2016 M.J. Pennington/ Orange Angels Studio

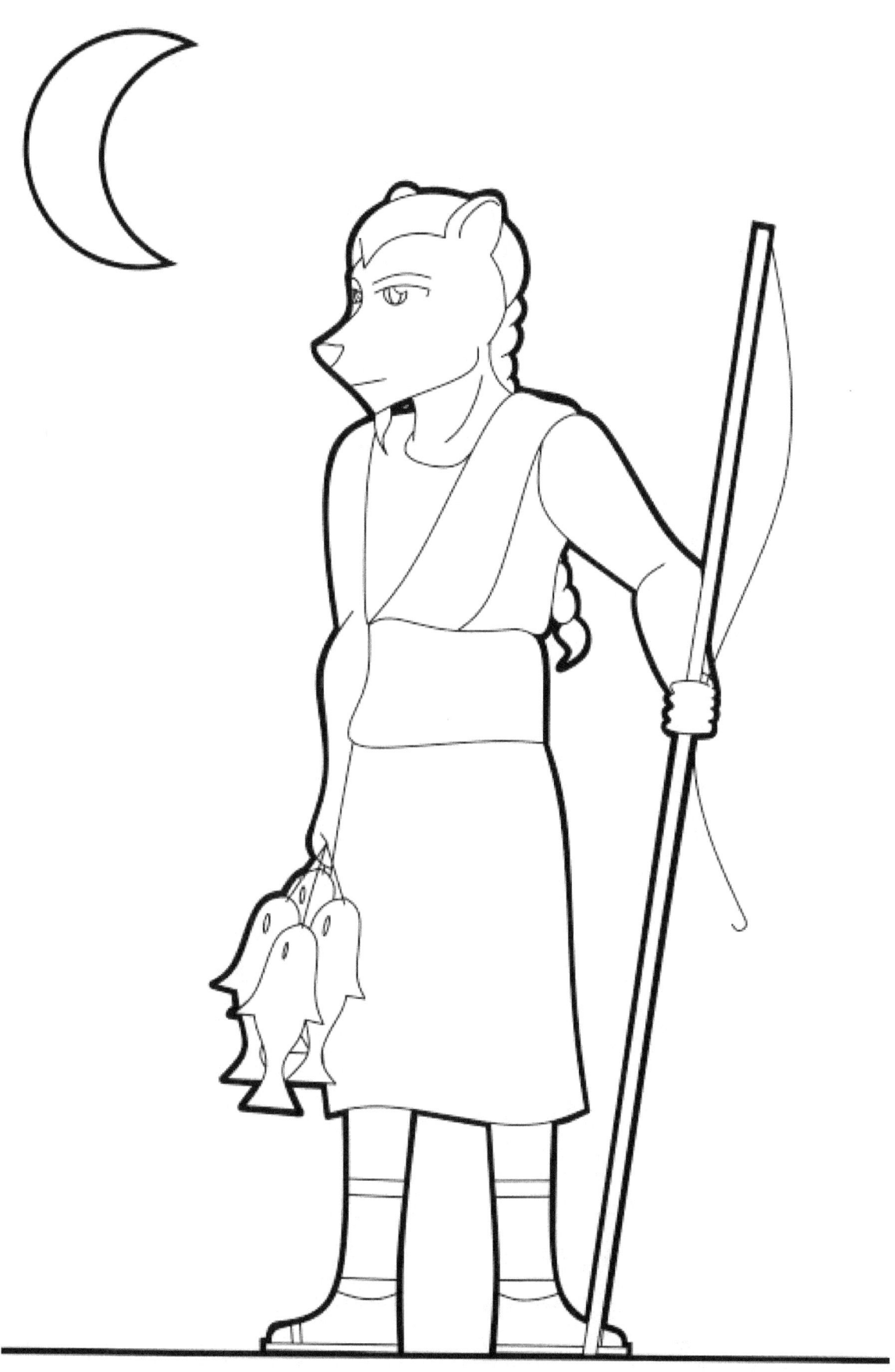

the Night Fisherman © 2016 M.J. Pennington/ Orange Angels Studio

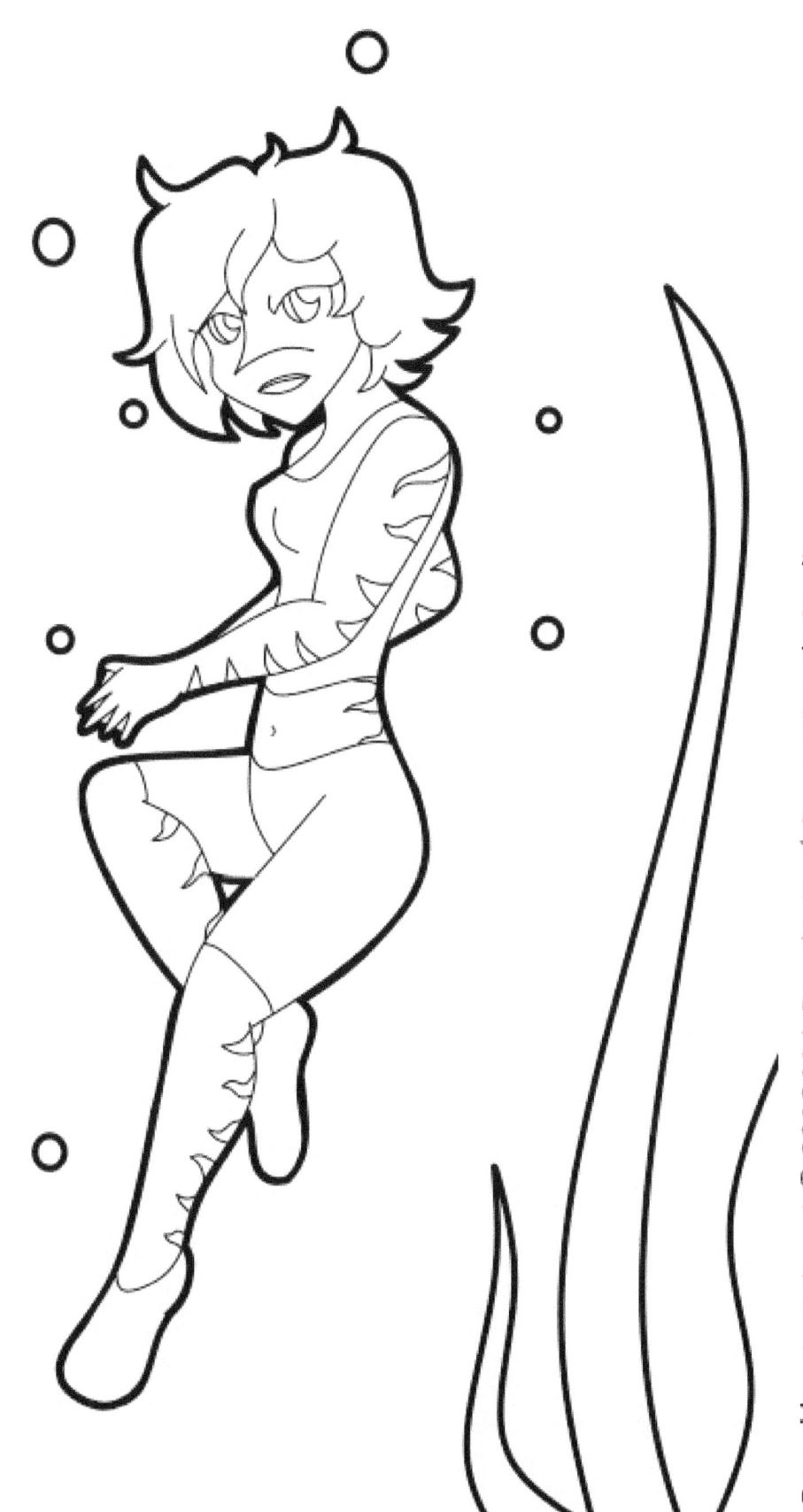

TIGRIS GALDEAN IS
THE PURRFECT AGENT
A BLUEPOOL STUDIO PRODUCTION

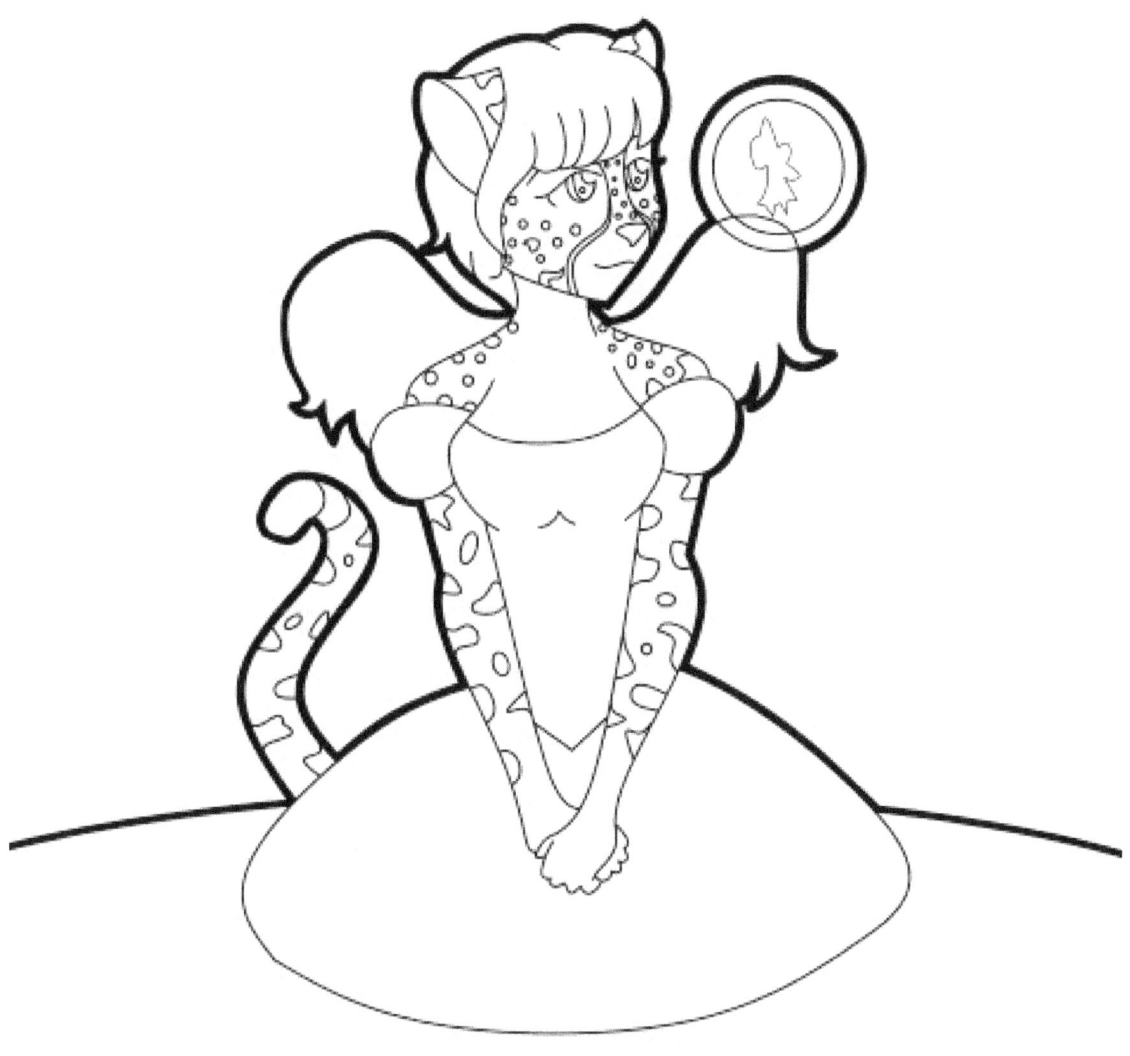

She dreams of more than running © 2016 M.J. Pennington/ Orange Angels Studio

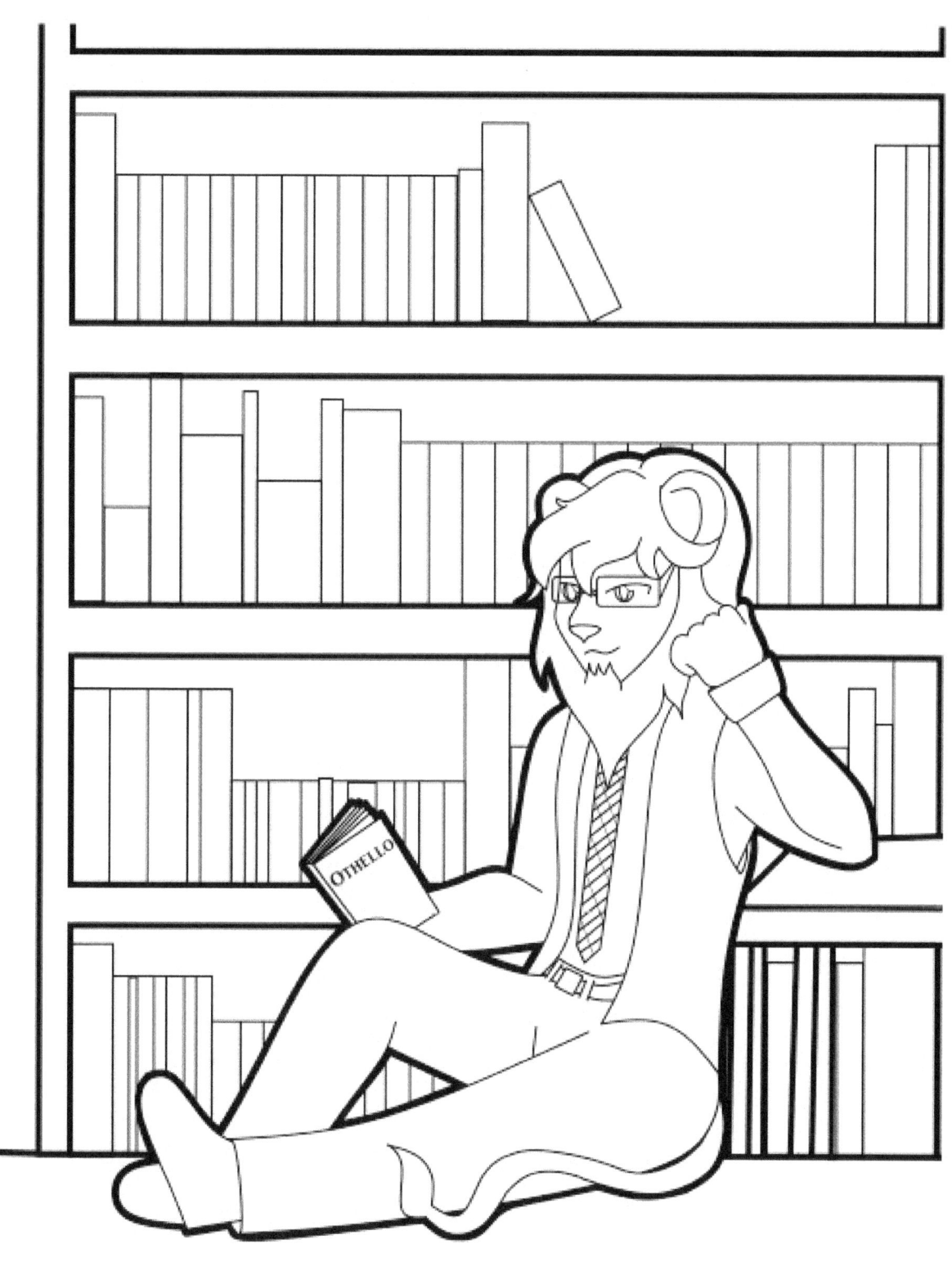

He does more than just guards © 2016 M.J. Pennington/ Orange Angels Studio

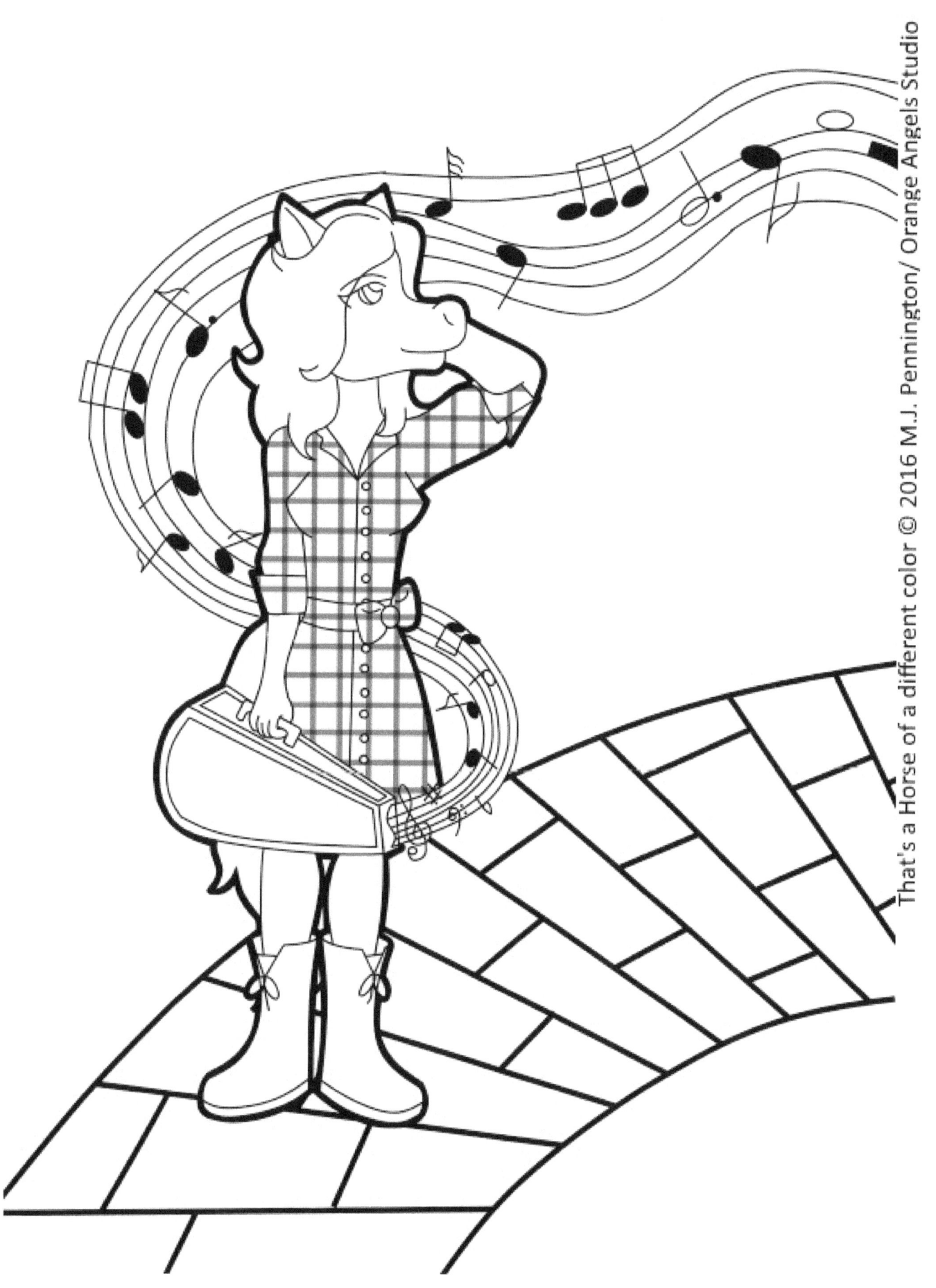

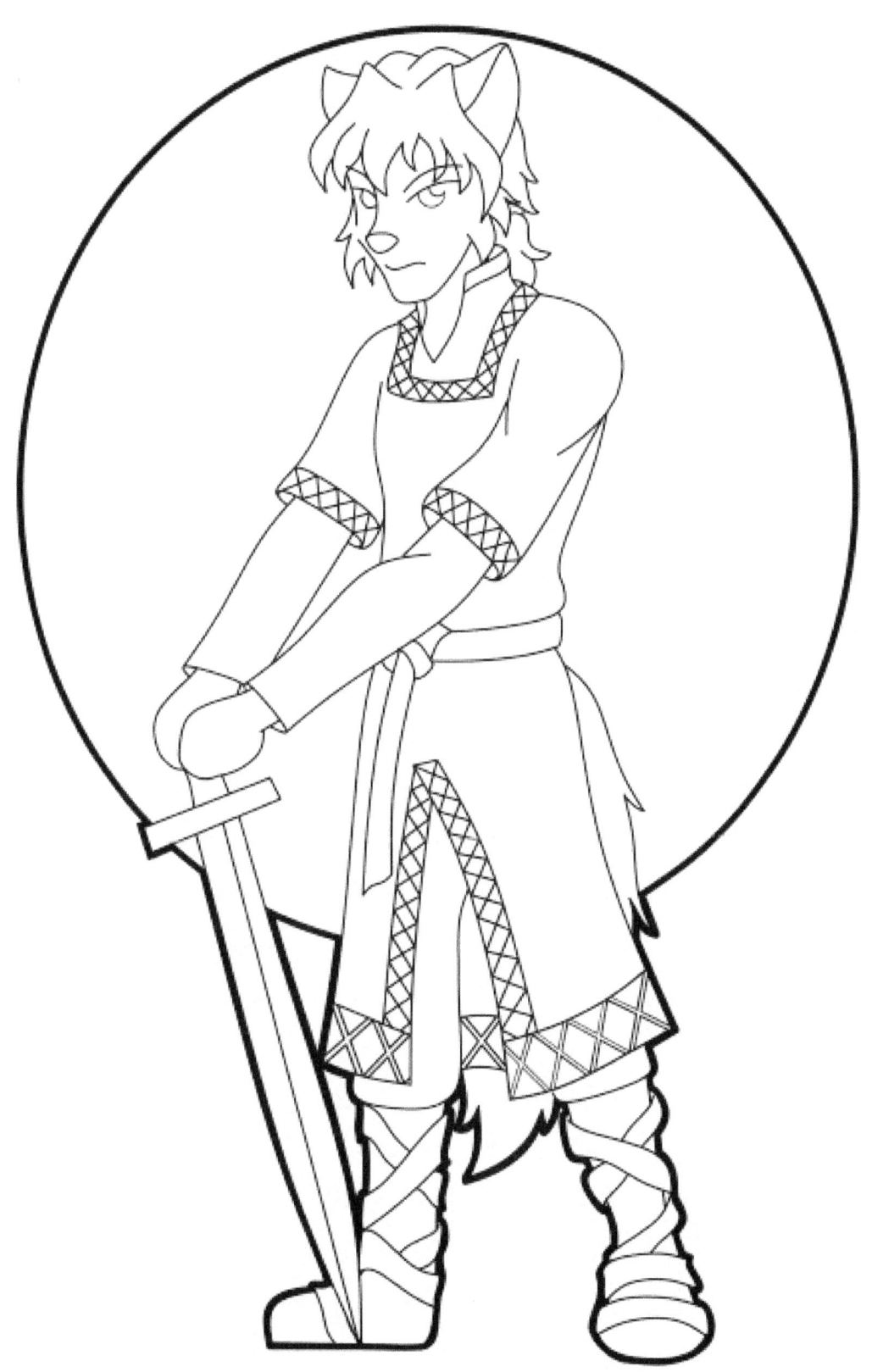

Dog of Denmark © 2016 M.J. Pennington/ Orange Angels Studio

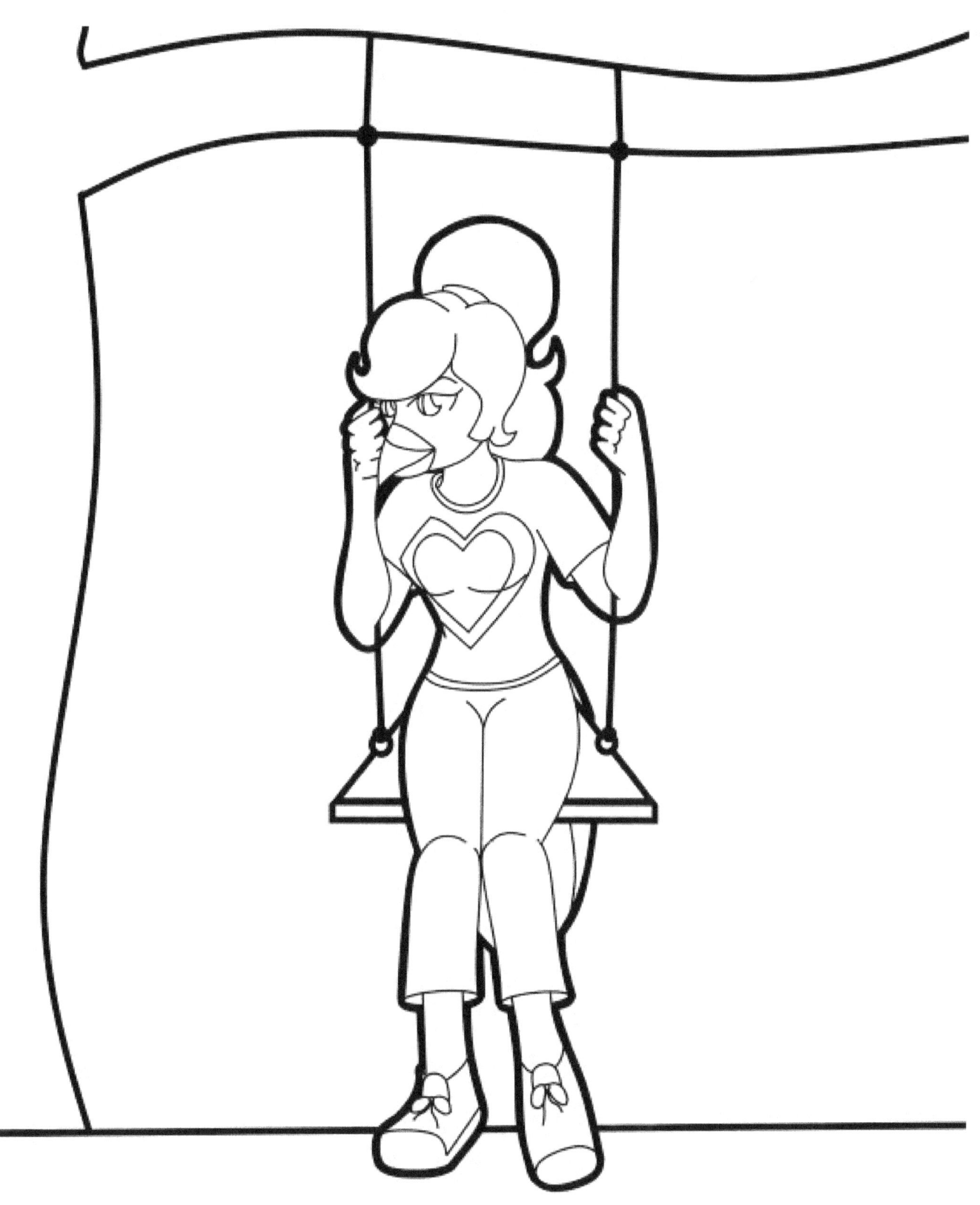

Sweet little Pigeon © 2016 M.J. Pennington/ Orange Angels Studio

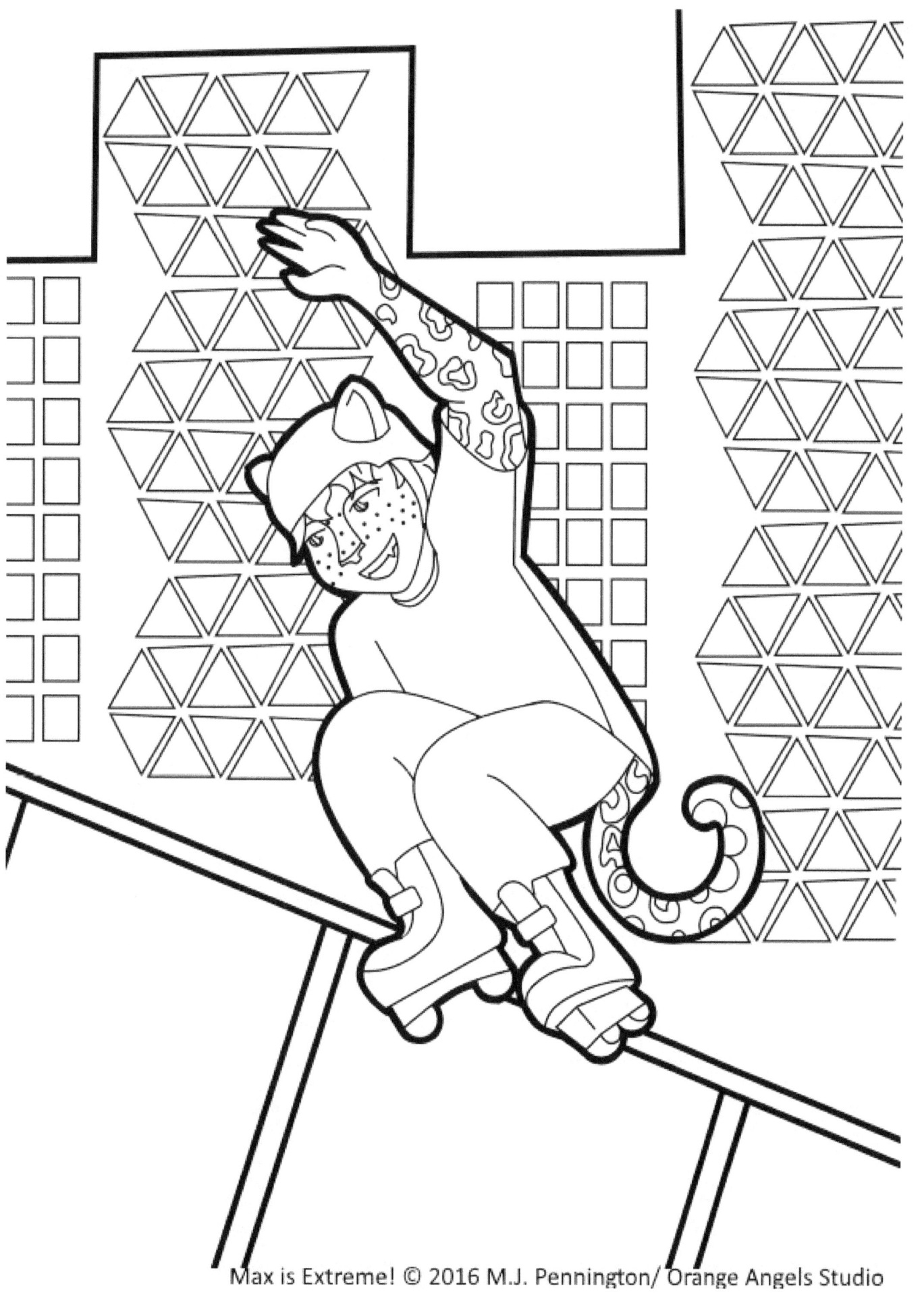

Max is Extreme! © 2016 M.J. Pennington/ Orange Angels Studio

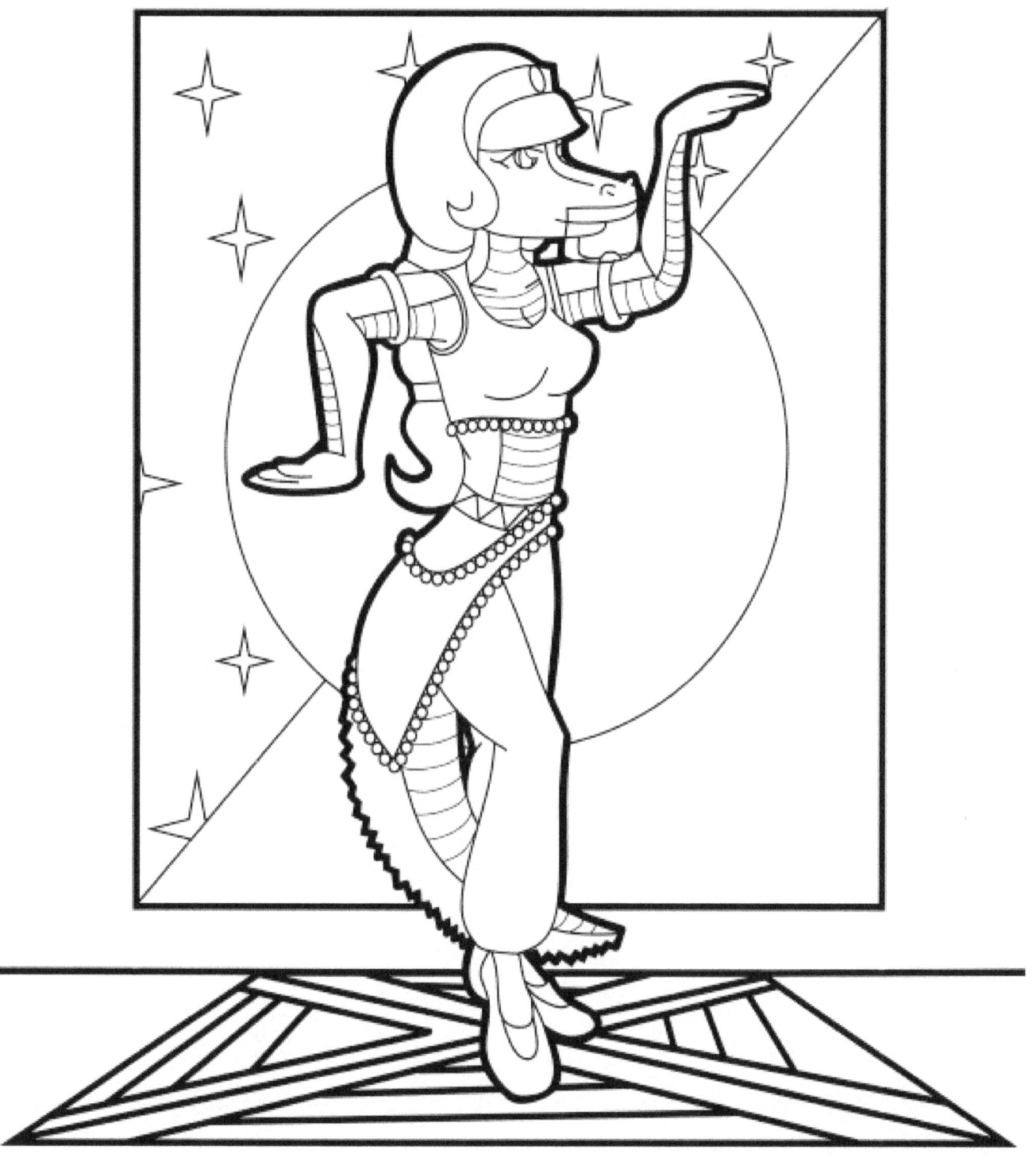

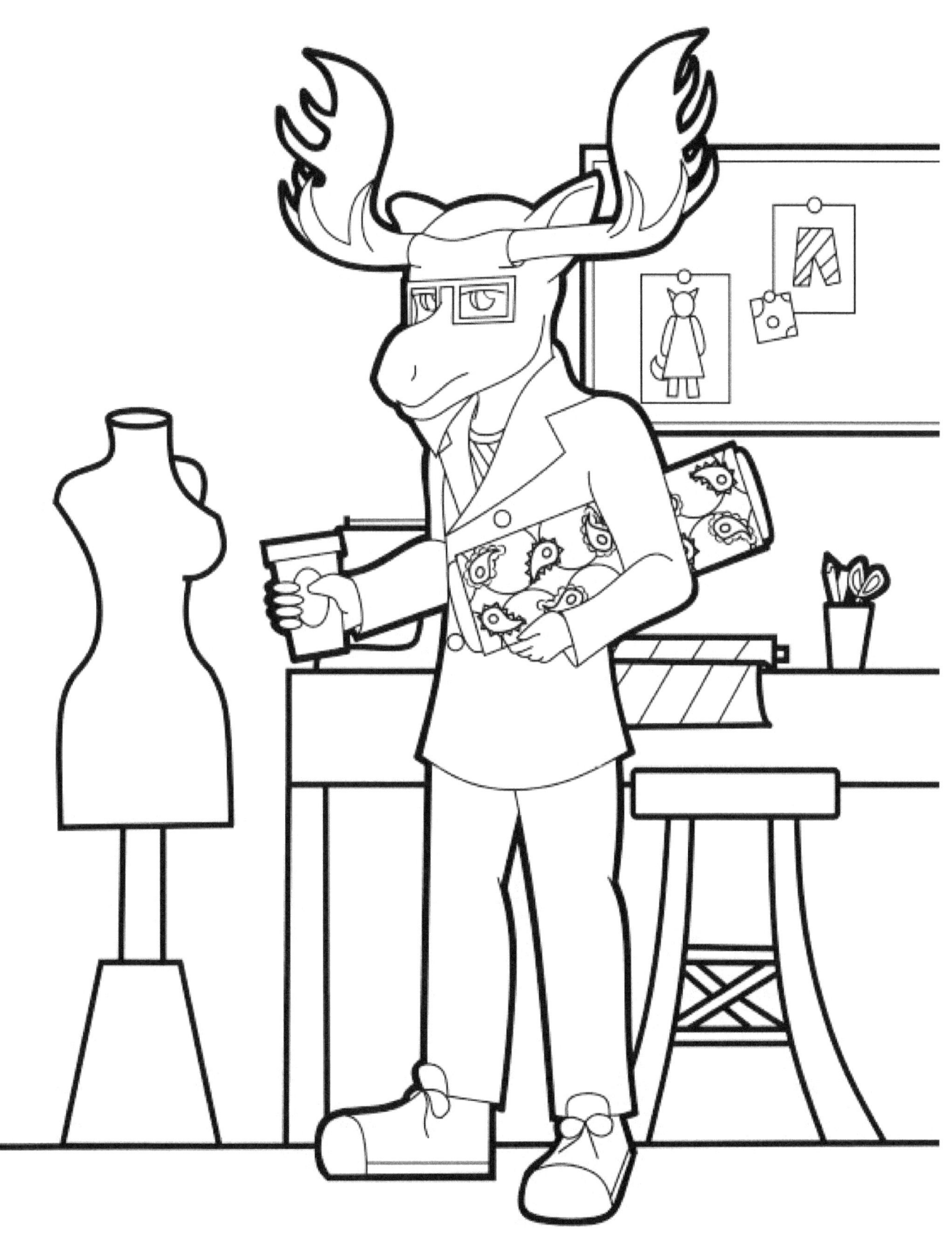

Moosemore Fashions © 2016 M.J. Pennington/ Orange Angels Studio

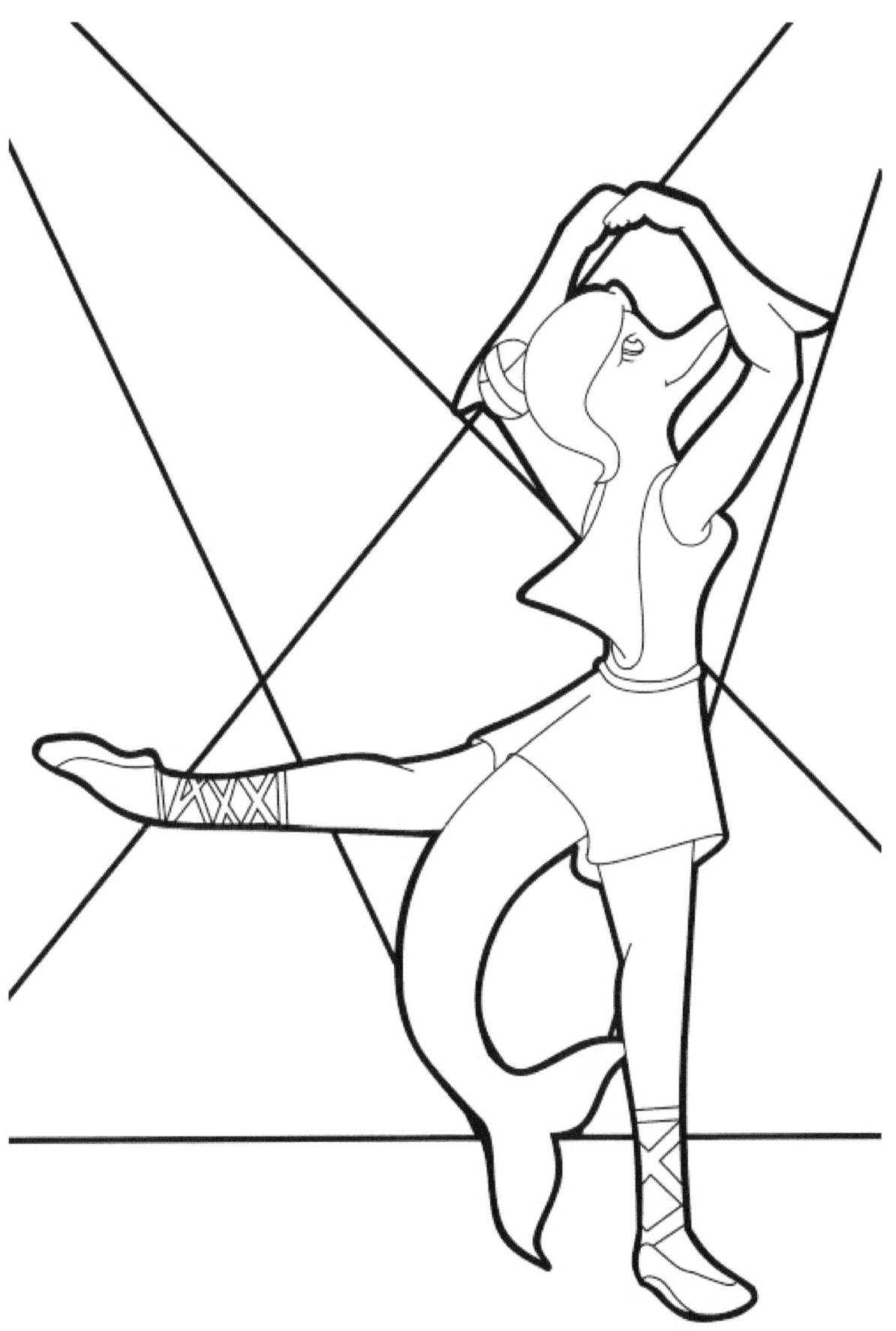

The Delightful Dolphin © 2016 M.J. Pennington/ Orange Angels Studio

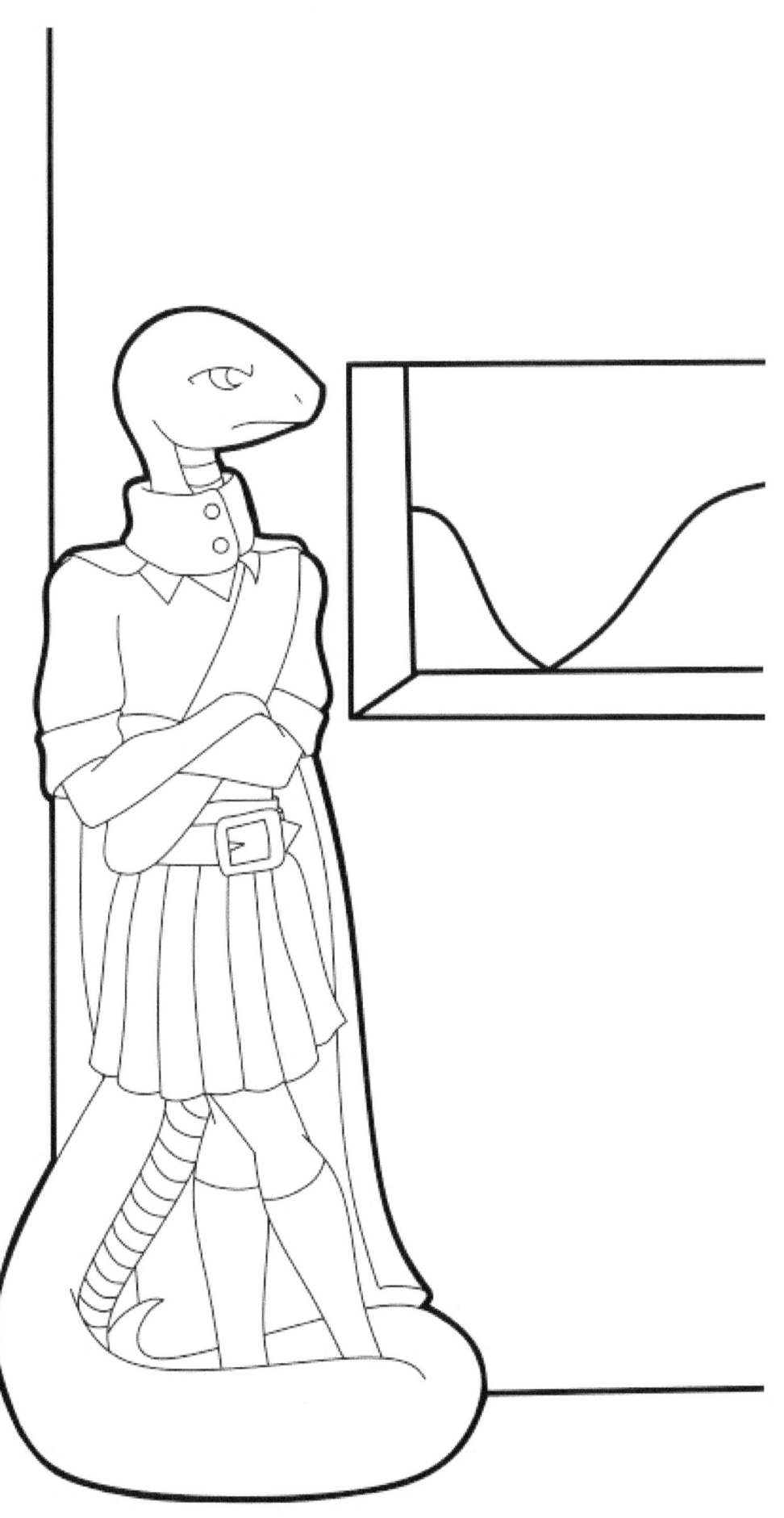

There is a snake in my Kilt © 2016 M.J. Pennington/ Orange Angels Studio

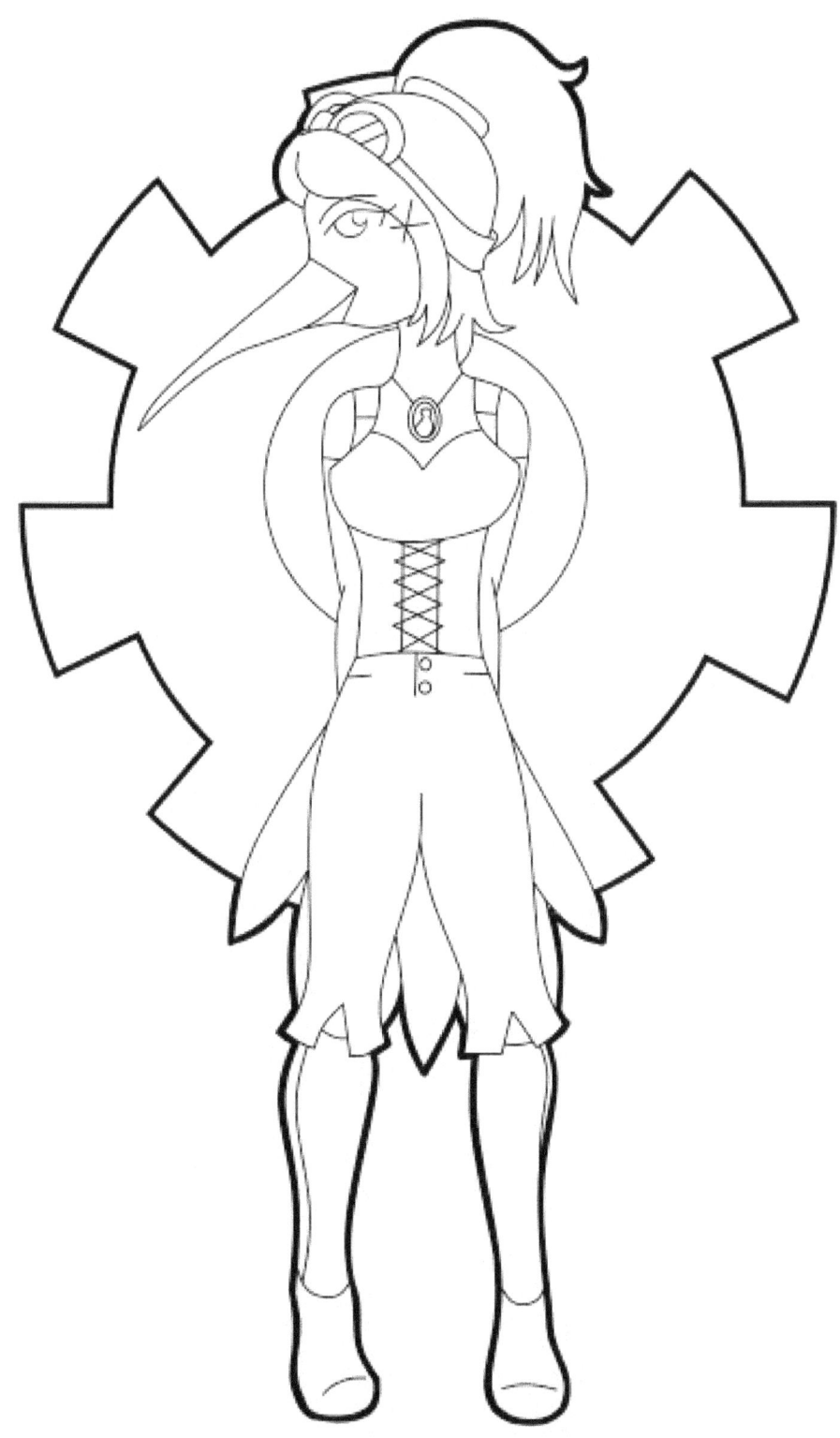

ABOUT THE ARTIST

M.J. Pennington

M.J. is a mom, artist, photographer, and cosplayer.

If you like this coloring book feel free to check out
her pictures and other artwork on her studio page.

Orange Angels Studio
www.facebook.com/OrangeAngelsStudio